IMAGES OF A GOLD

Dutch Seventeenth

FOR ROSA

Images of a Golden Age

Dutch Seventeenth-Century Paintings

Christopher Wright
Edited by Richard Lockett

Birmingham City Museums
and Art Gallery

First edition 1989

Published by
Birmingham City Museums and Art Gallery
Chamberlain Square
Birmingham B3 3DH

on the occasion of the exhibition

IMAGES OF A GOLDEN AGE
DUTCH SEVENTEENTH-CENTURY PAINTINGS
7 October 1989–14 January 1990

Produced for the Birmingham City Museums and Art Gallery by
Lund Humphries Publishers Ltd
16 Pembridge Road London W11 3HL

British Library Cataloguing in Publication Data
Wright, Christopher, *1945–*
[Dutch painting in the seventeenth century]. Images of a golden age: Dutch seventeenth-century paintings.
1. Dutch paintings – Catalogues, indexes
I. [Dutch painting in the seventeenth century] II. Title
III. City Museums and Art Gallery, *Birmingham, England*
759. 9492′ 074

ISBN 0 7093 0162 6

Designed by Alan Bartram
Made and printed in Great Britain by
BAS Printers Limited, Over Wallop, Hampshire

A casebound version of this catalogue, which also includes a complete list of Dutch seventeenth-century artists represented in British public collections, The Royal Collection, The National Trust and The National Trust for Scotland (including artists active in the Dutch Republic in the seventeenth century, not represented in British public collections) is published by Lund Humphries Publishers Ltd under the title *Dutch Painting in the Seventeenth Century* (ISBN 0 85331 563 9)

Contents

List of Illustrations

Foreword and Acknowledgements

The motive for the exhibition, to which this book is related, was straightforward, to allow visitors to the Birmingham City Museum and Art Gallery a brief opportunity to enjoy the achievement of Dutch 17th-century painters. This is in the knowledge that their 'images of a golden age' can capture the interest of a wide and popular audience. This popularity no doubt reflects the fact that Dutch artists had to be responsive to a new market force, patronage that was directly or indirectly drawn from a much wider spectrum of society than in the past. Many of us share the same delight in precise description of the physical world as epitomised by the Dutch still-life and are persuaded that many landscape paintings are accurate and unidealised descriptions of Dutch landscape, weather and all.

Sadly, the British taste for Dutch pictures is not adequately mirrored in Birmingham's permanent collection which is founded on gifts made to the City from the mid-19th century onwards; chance, one feels, might well have dealt the cards differently. Of the eight or so Dutch 17th-century paintings acquired before 1945, only one could be described as significant, two are good of their kind but of minor importance, two more are of low quality while two, a 'Berchem' and a 'Hobbema' are probably 18th-century pastiches. Post-1945 curator-led collecting might have created a strong Dutch school but chose instead to favour the 17th-century Italians. The motive has therefore been to redress the balance for a moment and in order to present a balanced view a general perspective has been taken rather than a concentrated look at one kind or genre of Dutch painting which has been done through some spectacular international exhibitions in recent years. Within this framework an attempt has been made to separate out the special character, where it exists, of the principal centres of production and to express something of the range and variety of work 'for sale' there.

Ninety per cent of the 143 paintings brought together here come from British public collections and this selection is in some sense a sample of Dutch pictures to be found in museums and galleries from Dundee to Southend. Christopher Wright and I have visited over forty galleries in order to view wherever possible all holdings relevant to the verification of pictures listed here as 17th-century Dutch as well as to select pictures for the exhibition. Those familiar with the limited facilities for storage afforded to many museums in this country and who are aware of the increasing frequency with which Old Masters are required to give way to contemporary display priorities, will appreciate the difficulty of conducting an informed survey where scholarly catalogues do not exist. In addition to the museological experience gained from joint expeditions I would like to acknowledge the enhanced understanding of Dutch painting that I owe to Christopher Wright.

We both owe a considerable debt to those museum directors, curators, conservators and other staff who made their collections accessible as well as to those who have loaned or prepared for loan the pictures illustrated here. I am conscious that the lists of those we wish to thank, long as it is, cannot be comprehensive:
Noël Annesley, Jane Baker, Richard Barker, Diane Barre, John Barwick, Jonathan Benington, Chloe Bennett, Vivienne Bennett, Marcus Bishop, Hilary Blume, Susan Bourne, Patrick Boylan, John Bradshaw, George Breeze, Christopher Brown, Julius Bryant, Anne Bukantas, Charlotte Burri, Tom Caley, Francis Cheetham, Michael Clarke, Reg Clarke, Timothy Clifford, Elizabeth Conran, David Cordingly, Bryan Crossling, John Crowder, Melissa Dalziel, Peter Dawson, Patrick Day, Anne Donald, Timothy Egan, James Estell, Mark Evans, Brendan Flynn, David Fraser, Rosalind Freeman, Anne French, Trevor Galloway, Christopher Gilbert, Mike Goodall, Victor Gray, Lynn Green, Richard Green, Francis Greenacre, Ann Gunn, Vivien Hamilton, Frances Hazlehurst, Gill Hedley, Geoffrey Henderson, Elizabeth Holford, Martin Hopkinson, Bryan Hughes, Clive Humphrey, Lucy-Anne Hunt, James Hunter, John Jacob, Michael Jaffé, Adrian Jenkins, David John, Nicola Kalinsky, Alastair Laing, Jennifer Lambert, C Leeming, Lionel Leventhal, Sir Michael Levey, Christopher Lloyd, James Lomax, Kate Lowry, Hugh Macandrew, Neil MacGregor, Duncan McMillan, David McNeff, Sandra Martin, Henry Middleton, Hamish Miles, Sir Oliver Millar, James Miller, Barbara Milner, Andrew Moore, Jim Morgan, David Morris, Edward Morris, Jane Munro, Brian Murray, Simon Murray, Gill Nock, Claire Nunns, Robin Paisey, Sue Parkes, Nicholas Penny, Roger Quarm, Alison Redwood, John Rhodes, Philip Richardson, Joanna Rickards, Hubert Rigg, R Riley, Alexander Robertson, Jill Robinson, Anne Robson, Joe Rock, Robin Roger, Barley Roscoe, Ian Scott, David Scrase, Jill Shield, Claire Slattery, Julian Spalding, Sarah Staniforth, Timothy Stevens,

Margaret Stewart, Sheena Stothard, Ann Sumner, Eric Taylor, John Taylor, Stephanie Teychenne, Norman Thomas, Veronica Tonge, Julian Treuherz, Philip Vainker, Neil Walker, Jean Walsh, Giles Waterfield, Jeffrey Watkin, Louise West, Jon Whiteley, Kathy Williams, Heather Wilson, Clara Young and my colleagues in all departments at the Birmingham City Museums and Art Gallery.

Several of the great names of Dutch painting would not have been included but for most generous loans from the Royal Collection by gracious permission of Her Majesty the Queen and from the National Gallery, London, by courtesy of the Trustees.

The List of Lenders (p.14) will demonstrate where the burden of support has otherwise fallen. A number of lenders have organised for conservation work to be carried out prior to loan. The granting of a Government Indemnity through the Office of Arts and Libraries has been crucial to the realisation of the project.

The Birmingham City Museums and Art Gallery gratefully acknowledge financial support towards this publication and the related exhibition from:
Algemene Bank Nederland NV
Birmingham City Centenary
Christie, Manson & Woods Ltd
Esmée Fairbairn Charitable Trust
IBM United Kingdom Ltd

RICHARD LOCKETT
Keeper of Fine Art
Birmingham City Museums and Art Gallery

Introduction

There is no parallel in western culture for the quality and quantity of painting produced in the 17th century within the small compass of the Netherlands. Until the present century no other school of painting has enjoyed so much esteem with the general public, although this interest could not be fed with much factual evidence about the lives of the artists concerned. Few details of most of the artists' lives survive besides legal actions, business transactions and records of births, marriages and deaths. These bare facts rarely build up to a convincing or accurate picture of even the greatest artists.

The richness of subject-matter and the variety of approach to be found in Dutch painting has been easily understood yet the very essence of the period has remained elusive. There is no overriding theme or single charismatic figure to epitomise the Dutch Republic in its golden age as there is for France in the person of Louis XIV. As a result Dutch painting has often been interpreted as a manifestation or extension of the social order in general. This approach has the advantage of explaining the subject-matter of Dutch art as far as recording the structure and attitudes of the society of the time, but it fails to explain the essence of art or what motivates and defines artistic genius.

Until the middle years of the present century the appreciation of Dutch 17th-century art consisted of an accumulation of previous likes and dislikes, and many distinguished painters who had enjoyed great reputations in their lifetimes were ignored because their work fell foul of 18th- or 19th-century canons of taste.

The approach taken here is to accept both the historical and the aesthetic points of view. Various methods have been tried in the past to divide painters into categories. There have been many specific studies of particular subjects, especially landscape, still-life and genre. This system has the weakness of losing the artistic personality of any individual who worked in several categories. As modern research proceeds many painters who were hitherto regarded as specialists are revealed as having painted competently in some or all the genres (see van den Eeckhout, pp.130f, 138f, for a good example of an artist using a totally disparate style according to the needs of the subject-matter). Rembrandt, perhaps the most various of all Dutch 17th-century painters, besides being primarily a painter of portraits and religious pictures, also painted still-life, landscape and genre. Vermeer of Delft, the great genre painter, also produced the finest of Dutch townscapes in his *View of Delft* (The Hague, Mauritshuis).

By interpreting an artist's work exclusively in terms of social phenomena there is a loss of personal identity and a belittling of artistic achievement. This runs in the face of what we know about the passionate responses of the Dutch themselves towards individual achievement at the time. The evidence for this is not found in art criticism or theory – of which there is remarkably little – but in the sometimes enormous prices then paid for a named individual artist's work.

It can be equally dangerous to overemphasise particular artists such as Rembrandt, Hals and Vermeer of Delft, and to see the whole period as revolving round the great personalities of the time according to post-17th-century definitions. This view of Dutch painting has been applied particularly to Rembrandt so that his contemporaries have been characterised either as precursors of his achievement or pale reflections of his genius.

This entirely aesthetic approach to the past is often supported with fake historical justification. For example, Kenneth Clark placed Rembrandt on a pedestal in the name of cultural history by ignoring the historical fact that Rembrandt's contemporaries esteemed several painters far above him, including Gerrit Dou, Ferdinand Bol and Bartholomeus van der Helst. To ignore the aesthetic values of the period under study is to deny history and it is a harsh fact that our own values, often in reverse of those of the time, should not be used as a basis for the study of the period.

The method adopted here is to focus on the principal centres of painting within the Dutch Republic. Each city existed as a separate and largely self-governing entity as a result of the long evolution of the Netherlands as the most prosperous area of Northern Europe. Historically and culturally the area north of France which consisted of the seventeen Provinces of the Netherlands was a single entity. Only in the middle years of the 16th century was there a break caused by the Reformation as a result of which the Southern Provinces remained largely Roman Catholic and the Northern ones largely, but not exclusively, Protestant. As in other parts of Northern Europe, especially the German States, what had begun as a religious divide turned into conflict both religious and political. The Southern Provinces of the Netherlands with the main cities of Bruges, Antwerp and Ghent remained loyal to their Spanish overlords and many Protestants fled northwards to avoid the ever-increasing religious persecution. An act of rebellion against the Spanish, under the aegis of the inappropriately named William the Silent, united a number of the Northern Provinces against Spain. This brought into being a new nation – the Dutch Republic – which is usually seen to date from 1579, the year in which the Provinces of Holland, Zeeland and Utrecht formally united against Spain.

The newly formed State had a precarious existence against the efforts of the Spanish to regain control over the territory. The inhabitants of these rebellious provinces, conspicuously less wealthy than their southern counterparts, were able not only to hold the Spanish at bay but also to evolve a specific identity which soon became nationhood. Truce with Spain was signed in 1609 but peace was not finally achieved until 1648. The first years of the 17th century were for the Dutch ones of consolidation of their by no means securely held territory. Many institutions survived from the Middle Ages, in particular the jealously guarded rights and privileges of the larger cities. What emerged from this curious combination of religious and political turmoil and ancient traditions was the then unique constitution of the Dutch Republic. Seven of the seventeen Netherlandish Provinces were included in the Republic (Holland, Zeeland, Utrecht, Overijssel, Gelderland, Friesland and Groningen). In addition there were pieces of two more, Limburg and Brabant, which included the strategically important cities of 's-Hertogenbosch and Maastricht.

Each Province was virtually self-governing, as they had always been, but for mutual protection and benefit they each sent representatives to the central government which met in The Hague in the Province of Holland. The States General, as it was called, was only responsible for items of national interest, most notably defence against Spanish, or later French aggression. The highest military post (the Stadholder) was hereditary and remained in the family of the Princes of Orange throughout the century. The internal history of the Dutch Republic throughout the period is, therefore, the conflict between the cities which voted the money in the States General and the needs and ambitions of the Orange family.

It is a paradox that while Dutch domestic history of the 17th century remained at a level of internal conflict which never led to civil war, outside the Republic events were far more dramatic. It is one of the great surprises of history, both in economic and political terms, that the Dutch should have developed what was by the middle of the century a world Empire extending from the Americas to the Far East. They became the most powerful seafaring nation of the century and Amsterdam became one of the richest trading cities of the time, even outstripping Antwerp which had been the wealthiest city in the North in the previous century.

Unlike almost every other country in Europe at the time, Dutch society was essentially urban. The countryside mattered little, either socially or politically. The staple was fish rather than meat for the main urban centres, as all of them except Utrecht were close to water or virtually on the coast.

The idea that each main urban centre should have a readily identifiable artistic flavour is not a new one. Until the present century it was the custom for sale catalogues to indicate 'school of Leiden' or 'school of Haarlem'. To this day many art dealers describe themselves as dealers in 'Fine Paintings', a term which originated with the Leiden artists who were known as 'fijnschilders' (literally fine painters) because of their love for great or fine detail. This division by location has the merit of allowing the 17th-century historical framework to be viewed alongside contemporary taste. Though a very strong case can be made for the individuality of Haarlem, Utrecht, Leiden, Middelburg, Delft, Rotterdam and Dordrecht, no specifically 'Amsterdam' style can be defined. Artistic style cannot be seen as a unifying factor in Amsterdam – the city was far too cosmopolitan for that – but in other places the opposite prevails and what emerges in each main centre of population is a pattern of painting activity which is definable enough.

Each centre was able to support a specialist in each genre even though in most cases there was evidently a varied range of talent. Thus the flower painters of Middelburg and Utrecht excelled in the first part of the century but portraiture in both centres has either not survived or can be defined as comparatively weak. In the remoter and less wealthy provinces such as Friesland, the few painters active had to be more various in their approach in order to satisfy all local needs.

In studying each different centre – some of which, such as Haarlem and Amsterdam, were only a few miles from each other – one can note either the impact of leading painters or paradoxically the lack of it. Vermeer was virtually isolated in Delft as he did not have any distinguished or influential patrons. As a young man he was part of the great expansion of activity which produced the distinctive Delft style of the 1660s. In his glorious maturity, during which he painted *The View of Delft* (The Hague, Mauritshuis), one of the greatest pictures of the whole century, his influence on other artists, however, was minimal. The only detectable effect Vermeer had on his contemporaries was on the Rotterdam genre painter Ochtervelt, an influence recognised by many critics who have accordingly treated him only as a minor figure within the field of Dutch genre painting. Exactly the reverse is true of Rembrandt both in his early years in Leiden and in his later Amsterdam career. Rembrandt, partly through his pupils, had a widespread influence on several other centres, especially Dordrecht.

Most painters, however, fall between the two extremes of Rembrandt and Vermeer. Many of them adopted current artistic fashions in their youth and were unable to cope with the rapid changes which took place from the 1630s onwards (Cornelis van Haarlem and Roelant Savery for example). Sometimes they are innovators in a modest way and their achievements were built on by later generations (Jan van Goyen could never have developed without the example of Esaias van de Velde). Yet other artists were able to change with fashion, not always to advantage. Pieter de Hooch and Honthorst fall into this category and their later work is held in lower esteem today. However, at the time, Gerrit Honthorst, by responding to fashions, achieved a greatly enhanced international reputation and he was employed by the kings of Denmark and England.

It needs to be reiterated that artistic style mattered very much to the 17th-century Dutch. Collectors were very concerned with the finish of a painting, hence the rapid decline in van Goyen's reputation after *c.*1650 as collectors sought after more detail. Higher prices were paid for detailed pictures rather than large-scale ones. Thus the collectors, and to an extent the art market in general, dictated the way Dutch artists approached their subject, especially in the second half of the century when the art market became more highly developed.

Even though style played such an important part in the production of a picture, the historical, social, economic and scientific background to the Dutch Republic cannot be ignored in any assessment of the art of the period. Even a summary account should point out that the Dutch Republic has been consistently underestimated as an important model for several subsequent developments in European history. It was the first truly effective federal State (The United Provinces as it was properly called). It was the first truly *commercial* society based on trade and banking. It was the first modern State not to be dominated by a unifying figure. In the field of science and technology it led Europe throughout the century.

As far as the creation and collecting of art was concerned it was the increase in the wealth of the average citizen which allowed so many people to own works of art. The oligarchy which ruled the republic was largely made up of the merchant class which bought pictures as a trading commodity and did not commission works on a grand scale as did their French and Italian contemporaries. A few major decorative schemes commissioned for the Huis ten Bosch near The Hague or by the citizens of Amsterdam for their new town hall are the exceptions rather than the rule.

One of the least explored aspects of Dutch 17th-century art as a whole is that of artistic training. Remarkably little is known about it because nothing was ever written down. Early sources frequently give sufficient information to form some sort of artistic genealogy – who was the pupil of whom. This information can confirm a stylistic judgement, for example that Frans van Mieris was the pupil of Gerrit Dou. The reverse is true when it is noted that Abraham Bloemaert had a very large number of pupils, none of whom he influenced except his son Hendrick. Studio practice seems to have been a very personal affair without any specific academic rules. The guild system acted in a largely informal and haphazard way and did not restrict the travel of artists from centre to centre. The Guilds neither enforced long periods of apprenticeship nor regulated the age when an artist became old enough to sign his pictures.

Perhaps the single most important formative influence on Dutch painters from the end of the 16th century onwards was travel. This mostly took the form of a visit to Italy, usually via France rather than the Alps, and many Dutch painters went to Italy before *c.*1630. Vast quantities of engravings of Italian art also circulated in the North. The effects of the Italian experience were highly variable as can be seen by contrasting the work of Joachim Wttewael (p.43) or Jan Both (p.50). The number of pictures executed by Dutch artists while they were in Italy and their ability to satisfy the Italian demand for small cabinet pictures has been overlooked, but only a few of the pictures included here can be proved to have been painted in Italy – the best example being the miniature Italian landscape by Breenbergh (p.127). Dutch artists in Italy never formed an academy, preferring an informal club which became known as the 'Bentveughels'. They were fascinated by the Italian landscape and made many drawings of it. They were seduced by the dramatic lighting effects of a land much sunnier than their own. However, on return to the North they often changed their style of painting in order to satisfy their northern patrons.

Unlike most Italian painters the Dutch never saw art as an expression of an idea or theory. Elaborate allegories on the whole were avoided and proverbs or simple moral tales preferred. Even religious themes were treated more for their surface effect rather than for any deep insight into the significance of the event. In spite of the repeated contact with Italy there are no theoretical writings about art for most of the century. There are no records of what Frans Hals or Vermeer, for example, thought about art or each other. The fragment which survives of Rembrandt's writing is sufficiently ambiguous to imply that he troubled little with intellectual theorising. All this is in direct contrast to contemporary Italian and French painters who were passionately concerned with the theoretical and intellectual basis of their art. Those Dutch artists, and there were many of them, who travelled to France and the Italian City States, must have been aware of these essential differences in approach, but it seems that they remained unaffected by them. This no doubt reflects the different nature of patronage in the Netherlands. The Dutch bourgeoisie was interested in possessions rather than ideas and neither Church nor State were involved in significant commissions as in most other European States.

Recent scholarship has explored the interpretation of many Dutch pictures as commentaries on material possessions. Some of them, but by no means the larger proportion, contain either obvious or partly concealed warnings about the vanity of material things. This undercurrent reflects a conflict between the personal austerity preached by the Dutch Protestant Churches and the conspicuous consumption of the richest city of the time, which Amsterdam had become. The fact remains that whatever the moral implications of some pictures, most Dutch paintings of the period show an uninhibited delight in material possessions.

In artistic terms, the real beginning came in the 1580s with the revival of artistic activity after the uncertain years of the iconoclastic crisis. This was especially obvious in Haarlem and Utrecht. The revival of art coincided almost exactly with the first steps of the Northern Provinces of the whole Netherlands to unite in rebellion against Spanish rule. The re-emergence of painting in these beleaguered northern provinces is surprising enough since Leiden, Haarlem and Alkmaar each suffered spectacular sieges, remembered to the present day, which were particularly destructive.

The styles adopted at first were provincial imitations of those prevailing in the much richer provinces of the Southern Netherlands, especially of Antwerp. Antwerp remained under Spanish rule without toleration for Protestants. Considerable migration northwards followed which brought the Hals family from Antwerp to Haarlem, the Bosschaerts to Middelburg and Roelant Savery eventually to Utrecht.

Native painters in both Utrecht and Haarlem adopted a style which modern art history has defined as Mannerism. This definition was created for Italian art between the end of the Renaissance and the emergence of the Baroque. It has been applied somewhat uneasily to the Dutch and is a clear enough illustration of the dangers of classification by artistic style. The chief painters were Cornelis van Haarlem, Karel van Mander and Hendrick Goltzius in Haarlem and Abraham Bloemaert and Joachim Wttewael in Utrecht. Their work is unified by a similar sense of drawing, colour and scale. These did not form the basis of future 17th-century developments and so Cornelis van Haarlem, Bloemaert and Wttewael, who all lived well into the 17th century, became outmoded.

Portraiture, an important branch of Dutch painting, had its origins in these years. Already in the last years of the 16th century, group portraiture had been revived. Although portraiture was not to suffer the iconoclastic disruption of the mid-16th-century, the Truce with the Spanish in 1609 nevertheless gave a great boost to portrait painting since the militia companies, which had grown up in every centre of population both large and small, found themselves at leisure to commission group portraits.

When the struggle for independence against the Spanish was finally won in 1648 (Terborch's depiction of the events is in the National Gallery, London), there was a further expansion of painting activity. With the increase in the number of pictures produced their surface area became in general smaller. This was because such pictures were better adapted to the small houses of the increasingly wealthy merchant class.

The main centres, especially Amsterdam, were subject to quite rapid and sometimes radical changes of fashion which would have the effect of rendering a particular artist's style virtually obsolete. By the same token a type of art, hitherto either avant-garde or practised in a provincial centre, would suddenly become fashionable. Realistic landscape painting, for example, did not flourish in the 1660s as it did in Haarlem, but this situation changed when the great Jacob van Ruisdael moved from Haarlem to Amsterdam. Hobbema, a pupil of Ruisdael in Amsterdam, expanded and continued his master's style in later years.

The period of greatest artistic activity in the Netherlands was the 1650s and 1660s, especially in Delft, Haarlem and Amsterdam – Utrecht had enjoyed its greatest period of productivity in the 1620s and 1630s – and it is these two decades to which the term golden age can most properly be applied. Far-reaching changes took place in all the main centres in the 1670s as fashions tended dramatically towards French influence. This change began before the French military invasion of 1672. This invasion was repulsed by the Dutch but, it is now apparent, at great cost to the economic infrastructure of the Dutch Republic. However, the last years of the century saw no debacle. Politically the Dutch Republic entered a period of international power and prestige and the Stadholder Willem III was invited to occupy the English and Scottish thrones. For the first time numbers of Dutch painters enjoyed international reputations. Godfried Schalcken accompanied Willem III to England and Adriaen van der Werff entered the service of the Elector Palatine at Düsseldorf. Soon after his death Rembrandt's pictures began to enter European royal and ducal collections. Dutch art was collected with passion by German and Italian princes and there was no discernible decline in demand. To modern eyes it is curious that the artist making the highest prices at that time was van der Werff rather than any of the painters held in the highest esteem today.

By the time that the painter Houbraken compiled artists' biographies in the 1720s, Dutch painting was already on the decline both in output and inventiveness. Even though a proper history of Dutch art in the 18th century remains to be written, it is clear that the number of truly significant figures was very much smaller than in the previous century.

The richness and variety of Dutch 17th-century painting has always defied generalisation. It attracts categorisation much to the detriment of its aesthetic qualities. The achievement of the individual must never be underestimated in the search for the vision of the unified whole. Each painter in his time was esteemed for his specialist contribution, however small that may now appear to be. Paradoxically it was the great painters of the period who suffered more at the hands of their contemporaries who were not able to appreciate the various nature of their achievements. The most striking example of this was Rembrandt who was only esteemed by his contemporaries for particular aspects of his art. His most experimental pictures, most notably his freely brushed late works, were not admired. Vermeer did not find great success in Delft except with one passionate collector who owned twenty-two paintings by him. Present-day taste is often preoccupied with individuality rather than conformity and it is the exception from the accepted standard which often attracts. It is the unusual which has become famous – Hobbema's *The Avenue* (London, National Gallery), Vermeer's *View of Delft* and Frans Hals' *Laughing Cavalier* (London, Wallace Collection) to name a few of the most celebrated examples.

The selection of pictures for this survey has been based on several criteria, not least a search for the typical rather than the outstanding. An attempt has been made to view the painting activity of each centre in the context of the *general* level of achievement rather than to make a selection of the masterpieces of the period. Different levels of skill are brought together, ranging from the modest topography of Johannes Meerhout's *View of Gorinchem* (p.75) to the sublime treatment of light in Aelbert Cuyp's *View of Dordrecht* (p.122).

Interpretation of the real achievements of the Dutch 17th century remains consistently personal. There is no consensus such as unites the appreciation of the Renaissance. Even though it is unlikely that there will be a radical reassessment of the period as a whole, some adjustments are both inevitable and in the process of taking place. The Italianates have been reinterpreted and the precursors of the main achievements, especially those painters active in the 1620s, are now being rehabilitated. Even the most balanced view of the period is bound to contain subjective views which prove the inexhaustible depth of the Dutch achievement.

List of Lenders by Location

HER MAJESTY THE QUEEN
ter Brugghen Cat.8; Dou Cat.24; de Hooch Cat.82; Metsu Cat.25

BARNARD CASTLE, BOWES MUSEUM
Breenbergh Cat.106; van der Croos Cat.32; Willaerts Cat.6

BARNSLEY, CANNON HALL
van Everdingen Cat.52; van der Heyden Cat.139; van der Neer Cat.123; Netscher Cat.36; Adriaen van de Velde Cat.131

BARNSLEY, COOPER ART GALLERY
van der Heyden Cat.138; Savery Cat.3

BATH, HOLBURNE MUSEUM
Jacob Backer Cat.109; Berchem Cat.64; Benjamin Cuyp Cat.97; Maes Cat.102; van Poelenburgh Cat.12; de Vois Cat.34

BIRMINGHAM, BARBER INSTITUTE
de Gelder Cat.103

BIRMINGHAM, CITY ART GALLERY
Amsterdam school Cat.104; Bramer Cat.80; Gael Cat.74; van Goyen Cat.23; van Nickelen Cat.79; Ochtervelt Cat.92; Stomer Cat.9; Willem van de Velde II Cat.134; van Vries Cat.73
Private loans: van de Cappelle Cat.117; Aelbert Cuyp Cat.100; Frans Hals Cat.54; Jacob van Ruisdael Cat.130

BOLTON, ART GALLERY
Colonia Cat.93

BRIGHTON, ART GALLERY
Lievens Cat.22; Maes Cat.101; van der Neer Cat.126; Toorenvliet Cat.29; Esaias van de Velde Cat.63

BRISTOL, CITY ART GALLERY
Codde Cat.107; van der Heyden Cat.140; Frans van Mieris I (attributed) Cat.26; Jacob van Ruisdael Cat.68; Wijnants Cat.72

BURNLEY, TOWNELEY HALL
van Bijlert Cat.10

CAMBRIDGE, FITZWILLIAM MUSEUM
Denysz. Cat.87; Lachtropius Cat.136; Marseus van Schrieck Cat.135; Ruysch Cat.141; Verelst Cat.35; van Walscapelle Cat.137

CARDIFF, NATIONAL MUSEUM OF WALES
van den Eeckhout Cat.110

CHELMSFORD, SHIRE HALL
de Meyer Cat.91; Adriaen van Ostade Cat.61; van Tol Cat.28

CHELTENHAM, ART GALLERY
Sorgh Cat.89; Verbeeck Cat.49; van Vliet Cat.85

COVENTRY, HERBERT ART GALLERY
de Heusch Cat.15

DERBY, ART GALLERY
van der Hagen Cat.33

DONCASTER, ART GALLERY
Private loan: Duifhuyzen Cat.90; Post Cat.69

DUNDEE, CITY ART GALLERY
van Beyeren Cat.121; Gillis Claesz. d'Hondecoeter Cat.5

EDINBURGH, NATIONAL GALLERY
Jan de Bray Cat.56-59; Hobbema Cat.127

EDINBURGH, UNIVERSITY
ten Oever Cat.42; Pijnacker Cat.88; Steen Cat.27

EXETER, ROYAL ALBERT MEMORIAL MUSEUM
Leiden school Cat.20

GATESHEAD, SHIPLEY ART GALLERY
Adriaen Backer Cat.108; van der Croos Cat.65; van Delen Cat.17; Wttewael Cat.2

GLASGOW, CITY ART GALLERY
Hendrick Bloemaert Cat.11; van der Helst Cat.118; van der Werff Cat.95

GLOUCESTER, CITY ART GALLERY
van der Werff Cat.96

HULL, FERENS ART GALLERY
de Blieck Cat.18; Janssens Elinga Cat.122; Frans Hals Cat.55; Thomas Wijk Cat.70

KILMARNOCK, DICK INSTITUTE
Benjamin Cuyp Cat.98; de Lairesse Cat.142

LEAMINGTON SPA, ART GALLERY
Abraham Bloemaert Cat.1; Schalcken Cat.37; van de Venne (copy) Cat.31; Willaerts Cat.7

LEEDS, TEMPLE NEWSAM HOUSE
van Aelst Cat.86; Breenbergh Cat.105

LEICESTER, COUNTY MUSEUM AND ART GALLERY
de Heer Cat.47; van der Linde (attributed) Cat.45; Meerhout Cat.44; Salomon van Ruysdael Cat.66

LIVERPOOL, WALKER ART GALLERY
School of Rembrandt Cat.111, 112; Jan Victors Cat.133; van Vliet (formerly Royal Institution) Cat.84

LONDON, DULWICH PICTURE GALLERY
Hoet Cat.38, 39; Jan Weenix Cat.14

LONDON, GREENWICH, NATIONAL MARITIME MUSEUM
Porcellis Cat.21; Willem van de Velde I Cat.115; Vitringa Cat.48; de Vlieger Cat.116

LONDON, KENWOOD
Aelbert Cuyp Cat.99

LONDON, NATIONAL GALLERY
van den Eeckhout Cat.119; Rembrandt Cat.113; Vermeer of Delft Cat.83

MAIDSTONE, ART GALLERY
Schotanus Cat.46
Private loan : Schellincks Cat.132

MANCHESTER, CITY ART GALLERY
Houbraken Cat.143; Kalf Cat.120; Terborch Cat.41

NORWICH, CASTLE MUSEUM
Begijn Cat.30; van der Neer Cat.124

NOTTINGHAM, CASTLE MUSEUM
Dirck Hals Cat.53; Palamedes Cat.81; van de Venne Cat.16; Withoos Cat.43

NUNEATON, ART GALLERY
Savery Cat.4

OXFORD, ASHMOLEAN MUSEUM
Jan Both Cat.13; Coorte Cat.19

PETWORTH HOUSE (NATIONAL TRUST)
Hobbema Cat.128; Jacob van Ruisdael Cat.129

POLESDEN LACEY (NATIONAL TRUST)
van Everdingen Cat.51; van der Neer Cat.125; Terborch Cat.40

PRESTON, HARRIS MUSEUM AND ART GALLERY
Private loan : Dirck de Bray Cat.75,76

PRIVATE COLLECTION
Saenredam Cat.78

SOUTHAMPTON, CITY ART GALLERY
van Everdingen Cat.50; Koninck Cat.114
Private loan : Berckheyde Cat.77

SOUTHEND (WESTCLIFF) ON SEA, BEECROFT ART GALLERY
Molenaer Cat.71

UPTON HOUSE (NATIONAL TRUST)
Jacob van Ruisdael Cat.67

WOLVERHAMPTON, ART GALLERY
Hondius Cat.94

YORK, CITY ART GALLERY
Bega Cat.62; Jan de Bray Cat.60

List of Colour Plates

Plate I. Amsterdam school *Preparation for a Feast* [**104**]

Plate II. Abraham Bloemaert *Landscape with the Prodigal Son* [**1**]

I

II

Plate III. Mathias Stomer *An old Woman and a Boy by Candlelight* [**9**]

Plate IV. Frans Hals *A laughing Child holding a Flute* (*Sense of Hearing*) **[54]**

Plate V. Jan van Goyen *River Scene*, 1642 [**23**]

Plate VI. Pieter Codde *Dutch Cavaliers and their Ladies making Music*, 1631 [**107**]

V

VI

Plate VII. Pieter Jansz. Saenredam *Imaginary Church Interior* [**78**]

Plate VIII. Gabriel Metsu *The Cello Player* [**25**]

Plate IX. Pieter de Hooch *A Courtyard in Delft at Evening, a Woman spinning* **[82]**

Plate X. Jan van de Cappelle *Winter Scene* [**117**]

Plate XI. Aelbert Cuyp *View of Dordrecht, Evening* [**99**]

X

XI

Plate XII. Gerrit Dou *The Onion Chopper*, 1646 [**24**]
Actual size

Plate XIII. Bartholomeus van der Helst *Portrait of a Dutch Rear-Admiral*, 1662 [**118**]

Plate XIV. Abraham van Beyeren *Still-Life with Lobster, Fruit and China Ware* [**121**]

Plate XV. School of Rembrandt *The Angel appearing to Hagar* [111]

Plate XVI. Frans Hals *Portrait of a smiling Woman* [55]

Plate XVII. Adam Pijnacker
Mountainous wooded Landscape **[88]**

Plate XVIII. Jan Weenix *Landscape with a Shepherd Boy*, 1664 **[14]**

Plate XIX. Joris van der Hagen
Landscape with a Castle **[33]**

Plate XX. Roelof van Vries
Travellers by a Village **[73]**

XVII

XVIII

XIX

XX

Plate XXI. Jacob van Ruisdael
Winter Landscape [**130**]

Plate XXII. Willem van de Velde II
The English Ship, the 'Hampton Court' in a Storm [**134**]

XXI

XXII

Plate XXIII. Nicolaes Lachtropius *A Vase of Flowers* [**136**]

Plate XXIV. Hendrick Cornelius van Vliet *Interior of the Nieuwe Kerk at Delft*, 1667 [**84**]

Plate XXV. Johannes Vermeer of Delft *Young Lady at a Virginal* [**83**]

Plate XXVI. Hendrick ten Oever *Evening Landscape with a distant View of Zwolle*, 1675 [**42**]

Plate XXVII. Jan van der Heyden *Figures resting and promenading in an Oak Forest* [**140**]

XXVI

XXVII

Plate XXVIII. Matthias Withoos *Thistles and Butterflies* [**43**]

Plate XXIX. Godfried Schalcken *Self-Portrait by Candlelight* [37]

Plate XXX. Gerard Terborch *Portrait of Hendrick Casimir II, Prince of Nassau-Dietz* [**41**]

Plate XXXI. Adriaen van der Werff *St Margaret* [**96**]

Utrecht

From a purely visual point of view Utrecht remains the most spectacular of the main Dutch cities because it is still dominated by the vast tower of its cathedral. A number of other medieval churches also survive and, despite losses, it is still possible to recognise Utrecht as the chief ecclesiastical centre of the Northern Netherlands in the Middle Ages. It remained predominantly Catholic during the 17th century and this religious bias may well have determined the subject-matter of most Utrecht artists in the 17th century.

The painting tradition in Utrecht in the 16th century was certainly the strongest in all the Northern Netherlands under the leadership of Jan van Scorel. Scorel had accompanied the archbishop of Utrecht to Rome in 1522 when he had been elected Pope Hadrian VI and although his reign lasted less than two years it established a tradition of Utrecht artists visiting Italy which continued through the 17th century as well.

In almost all other Dutch centres there was a visible break in artistic tradition during the middle years of the 16th century, chiefly owing to Spanish sieges and iconoclasm. Utrecht seems to have escaped both and artistic tradition continued to flourish. Together with Delft and Leiden, Utrecht was among the largest of the Dutch cities until overtaken by Amsterdam in the early years of the 17th century. Utrecht painters were not apparently interested in their urban surroundings and the only memorable records of the appearance of the city are the church paintings of the Haarlem painter Pieter Jansz. Saenredam. There was no flourishing tradition of portraiture either, again unlike all the other main centres. Still-life paintings other than of flowers are rare too and the fish paintings of Willem Ormea, for example, are regarded as the lowliest of their kind. A search among quite minor painters is necessary in order to find representatives of all the genres.

The grand tradition of painting in Utrecht from the last years of the 16th century onwards is remarkably consistent both in style and subject-matter. The leading figures were Abraham Bloemaert and Wttewael (p.42) who took their style and subject-matter from Italian models. Both painters continued successfully well into the 17th century modifying their styles little so that by the end of their lives they were almost half a century out of date.

In the 1620s Utrecht was briefly in the forefront of Dutch painting. There can be no specific explanation for this sudden surge of innovation and activity and no other centre underwent such rapid changes before settling for a long static period. The inspiring event was the return from Italy of three painters, Baburen, Honthorst and ter Brugghen (p.47), all of whom were influenced to a greater or lesser degree by the art of Caravaggio and his followers. They are known generally as the Utrecht Caravaggesques despite some differences of artistic approach. Their choice of bold compositions, earthy subject-matter and extravagant lighting effects was short-lived and although often thought to typify the Utrecht School, relevant pictures are rare. Their influence on subject-matter and style in other centres has been consistently underestimated, but much history painting elsewhere and in Amsterdam in particular can be traced back to the work of these Utrecht painters. A specific example that can be cited is the dependence of Vermeer of Delft's earliest surviving picture, *Christ in the House of Martha and Mary* (Edinburgh, National Gallery), on the work of ter Brugghen.

The Caravaggesques went out of fashion as rapidly as they came in; ter Brugghen's art became much more individual and bland in tone and marks a return to Renaissance and even medieval inspiration. Honthorst's move towards a bland classicism was more influential and enabled him to acquire an international reputation from some large mythological or literary subject pictures. When Honthorst moved away from Utrecht this style was continued for a whole generation by Jan van Bijlert (p.48).

The dominance and importance of this mainstream has led many of the undercurrents to be overlooked, especially as they appeared to have little importance at the time. For example, the landscapes of Cornelis van Poelenburgh (p.49), who returned to Utrecht from Italy in the 1620s, appear modest enough but they were to set the model for a whole host of landscape artists for the rest of the century. The same is true of Jan Both (p.50) who influenced most other Italianate landscapists such as Berchem in Haarlem.

All these artistic styles, which are so easily recognisable, were imported fully-fledged from Italy and there was no local or native group of artists experimenting and influencing each other to create a major contribution to the mainstream of Dutch painting. Utrecht was the one centre where foreign, essentially Italian, influence continued largely undiluted to the end of the century.

The only truly local development was in the genre of flower painting in which Utrecht was a microcosm of the whole history of flower painting. Individual Dutch genres are notoriously difficult to categorise into a consistent development because of the cross-currents between different centres and influences from further afield. Suffice it to say that there was a preponderance of flower painters in Utrecht dating from the arrival of Roelant Savery and the visit of Ambrosius Bosschaert. From these two artists and their pupils evolved the style of the young Jan Davidsz. de Heem who then left for Antwerp. De Heem trained the German-born Abraham Mignon who became the chief representative of the mature Baroque flower piece. Almost all the other Dutch flower painters owe something to this clearly defined tradition and there is little evidence of such a specific local flavour developing in other centres.

Patrons seemed to have preferred larger-scale works and, apart from the inevitably reduced scale of flower pieces, there is a conspicuous emphasis on grand pictures in Utrecht. There is no evidence that the Catholics commissioned altarpieces for their churches, still vulnerable to iconoclasm, and most large religious pictures were intended for private devotion. The history of painting in Utrecht, therefore, does not accurately reflect Dutch achievements as a whole. The opposite is the case. Utrecht was dominated by foreign influences even though there was no special geographical reason for this.

Abraham Bloemaert
Gorinchem 1564 – Utrecht 1651

Along with his contemporary Wttewael, Abraham Bloemaert was the leading painter in Utrecht for almost two generations. Of all the painters who followed what modern art history (since the 1920s) has called Mannerism, Bloemaert was by far the most versatile both in approach and subject-matter. An inborn eclecticism allowed him to draw on a wide variety of sources both from Italian and Netherlandish art. Bloemaert's style of brightly-coloured and bold compositions changed little before the 1620s when he made certain modifications to accommodate the short-lived interest in Caravaggio. By the 1630s and 1640s his repetitions in his earlier manner were eighty years out of date but this did not seem to affect his success. He was important as a teacher; his sons, Hendrick and Adriaen, as well as Jan Both and Cornelis van Poelenburgh were among his pupils. He also had an influence on the 18th century, especially on François Boucher.

1 [colour plate II]

1. Landscape with the Prodigal Son
canvas; 105.4 × 163.8 cm
Warwick District Council Museum Service, Leamington Spa Art Gallery
This is a significant work in the history of the development of landscape painting in the Dutch Republic because it can be dated to *c.*1600 when it was engraved. Although one of the earliest landscapes painted in the North, it still belongs to the picturesque rather than to the realist tradition. The next generation of landscapists, and in particular Esaias van de Velde, was to experiment with the real effects of nature seen locally, features such as sand dunes and trees twisted by the wind. Bloemaert sought to create a complex decorative effect; the subject, the Prodigal Son, plays a very unimportant role and as the pitiful swineherd he is insignificantly placed on the right.

Joachim Anthonisz. Wttewael
Utrecht 1566 – Utrecht 1638

Wttewael was one of the most significant painters of his time in Utrecht. At the time of van Mander's *Het Schilder-Boeck*, published in Haarlem in 1604, Wttewael was still a young man but was given an honourable mention nevertheless by the first historian of Netherlandish painting. (Dutch artists had to wait until the early 18th century for another collection of artists' biographies and by that time much information had been lost.)

Wttewael was essentially a 16th-century artist who modified his style little once it had been formed. He worked on a large scale producing almost tapestry-like pictures with swirling figures and bright colour. His other manner, noted by van Mander, was used for incredibly detailed small pictures mostly painted on

2

copper (an example is at Waddesdon Manor). Wttewael was not an influential painter in the 17th century as style developed away from Mannerism, and by the early 1620s in Utrecht the influence of Caravaggio was attracting the younger generation of painters.

2. The Temptation of Adam, 1614
canvas; 164.5 × 110 cm
Shipley Art Gallery, Gateshead (Tyne and Wear Museums Service)
Wttewael's *The Temptation of Adam* is one of the most important Dutch Mannerist pictures in a public collection in the British Isles. Roelant Savery's pictures filled with his beloved animals lie behind this large-scale and ambitious picture. Such a picture marks the end of a tradition rather than the beginning of a new one and at the time of Wttewael's death in 1638 the styles and even subject-matter of both artists had become anachronistic.

Roelant Savery
Courtrai 1576 – Utrecht 1639

Savery was one of the most talented and influential of painters from the Southern Netherlands who made their careers in the Dutch Republic. Before migrating northwards his art had matured under the influence of Antwerp painters belonging to the Brueghel dynasty. He then spent a number of years in Prague (1604-16) working for the Emperors Rudolph and Matthias. He arrived in Amsterdam in 1616 and soon transferred to Utrecht where he spent the rest of his life. Savery's art can thus in no sense be considered Dutch as it was fully mature on arrival in the North. He made a number of subtle changes in emphasis as he grew older, almost certainly responding to the different demands of his Utrecht clients and to changing fashions in painting. Savery's importance as an influence on his Utrecht contemporaries needs emphasising. It was Savery, rather than Jan (Velvet) Brueghel, who was responsible for introducing the delicately-painted mountainous landscape still being produced as late as the 1680s by the Utrecht painter Herman Saftleven. Savery also painted a few highly refined still-lifes of pots of flowers which are derived from the Brueghel tradition. In common with his contemporary Wttewael, Savery worked both on a small and a large scale. For the small works he employed a miniaturist technique whereas the large pictures are tapestry-like in effect. The Hondecoeter dynasty of painters in Utrecht owed much to Savery's portrayal of animals.

3. Landscape with a Bridge
panel; 28.3 × 43.2 cm
Cooper Art Gallery Trustees, Barnsley Metropolitan Borough Council
This composition was engraved in reverse by Aegidius Sadeler as after Savery. The dating is more difficult to establish and it would be helpful to know whether this picture was executed before or after Savery arrived in the Dutch Republic. The general refinement and minutiae of technique, combined with the mountainous landscape subject, points to the possibility that this picture was executed while the artist was still in the service of the Emperor Rudolph in Prague. There are a number of rather similar pictures with early dates such as a pair of *Landscapes* dated 1608 (Hanover, Niedersächsisches Landesmuseum).

The strong blue-green tonality found in this picture was only adopted by a limited number of Dutch landscapists of the first generation. Most of them preferred the brownish tones of the local sand dunes rather than the artificial conventions of Savery.

3

4

4. Before the Deluge
canvas; 137 × 190 cm
Nuneaton Museum and Art Gallery
Savery rarely worked on such an ambitious scale as this and as a result there is some loss of finesse in the treatment of the details – the same is also true of Wttewael's work on a large scale. In general style and handling, the picture is likely to fall into the later part of the artist's career unlike the contrasted small-scale work at Barnsley (p.43). The story of Noah gave the artist the excuse to include a large number of animals and birds which he incorporates brilliantly into one of his standard wooded landscapes. The ark itself is only just visible in the background. Most of the animals and birds in the picture are remarkably well observed; they do not, on this occasion, include such exotica as the dodo.

Gillis Claesz. d' Hondecoeter

Antwerp ?*c.*1580 – Amsterdam 1638

In the search for the origins of Dutch landscape painting Esaias van de Velde has always been seen as the great precursor. In fact the work of Hondecoeter predates that of Esaias van de Velde by almost a decade, but Hondecoeter never developed beyond his initial achievement. The art of landscape painting as practised by the Brueghel family was fully mature in the Southern Netherlands (although, of course, it was to change direction dramatically under the influence of

5

Rubens) and Hondecoeter imported into the North a Flemish-based style modifying it in colour from the standard Flemish sharp browns, blues and greens. Most of the artist's career was spent in Utrecht and it is occasionally possible to detect the influence of Roelant Savery in his work, especially in his treatment of animals.

5. Landscape with the Expulsion of Hagar, 1609
panel; 57.8 × 75.6 cm
Reproduced here without the addition – see below
Dundee Art Galleries and Museums
Recent cleaning has confirmed the signature as Hondecoeter and the date on this picture as 1609 confounding the theory that this was a decade too early. The composition has been enlarged at the top, probably in the 18th century, in order to make the sky more acceptable to the taste of the time (the same happened to the Esaias van de Velde at Brighton (p.88)). The picture illustrates how Hondecoeter made an essentially Brueghel-inspired landscape softer, more subdued and more atmospheric. This was precisely the direction Esaias van de Velde was to take although he was to be much more various in his approach and hence much more influential. Hondecoeter had very little influence and landscape painting in Utrecht took on a quite different emphasis under the leadership of Cornelis van Poelenburgh.

Adam Willaerts
Antwerp 1577 – Utrecht 1664

Willaerts was one of the many artists to migrate northwards from his native Antwerp (Ambrosius Bosschaert, the Hals family and Roelant Savery being other examples) and he settled in Utrecht bringing with him an essentially Southern Netherlandish style. The source for Willaerts' style lies in the work of Pieter Brueghel and his pupils, sons and followers even though Willaerts developed a distinctive and easily recognisable style of his own. He was the only painter in Utrecht to specialise in seascape painting, but his pictures never became pure seascapes in the manner favoured by Hendrick Cornelis Vroom in Haarlem. Willaerts' output was considerable and his pictures have some interest today as he occasionally depicted the embarkation and disembarkation of members of the British Royal Family on their way to and from the

6

7

Netherlands (examples at Greenwich and in the Royal Collection). Most of the artist's work is on a generous if not large scale and he often favoured bright colours for his numerous figures. This tradition was not taken up by most other Dutch seascape painters and his work remained rather old-fashioned in the relative isolation of Utrecht.

6. Embarkation Scene, 1626
panel; 82.7 × 147.9 cm
Bowes Museum, Barnard Castle, Co. Durham
It is possible that this embarkation scene depicts a specific event despite the landscape appearing rather fanciful; it is certainly not meant to be a Dutch location. Clearly the people preparing to enter the boat are persons of some consequence and the artist has been careful to denote social status via costume. Even the people on the shore on the left appear to be of differing social classes. The fact that the picture is dated 1626 is of some interest as it demonstrates that the artist had not modernised his style to match changes taking place in such centres as Haarlem.

7. The Landing of Pilgrims, 1623 (or 1628)
panel; 34.5 × 54.2 cm
Warwick District Council Museum Service, Leamington Spa Art Gallery

This modest work (in comparison with the Willaerts from the Bowes Museum) follows a trend towards monochrome which had affected almost all Dutch landscape and seascape painters after the mid-1620s. For seascape this trend was led by Jan Porcellis (p.58). Two-thirds of this composition illustrates the new realism, but on the left the old drama is retained even if the piling-up of the buildings and figures is a little more low key. The subject – the landing of the pilgrims en route for the Holy sites – was more suitable for a Catholic than a Protestant patron.

Hendrick ter Brugghen

Utrecht *c.*1588 – Utrecht 1629

Recent study has revealed more details about ter Brugghen's early life, but there are still unsolved problems about how his art evolved and matured. It is documented that ter Brugghen spent a long period in Italy but came back to the North about 1614. Only one painting can be placed before 1620 with certainty and this, although large scale, is modest in achievement. The rest of ter Brugghen's paintings, many of them dated, must be crammed into the next nine years (1620-29). He is usually dubbed an 'Utrecht Caravaggesque' which only partly describes his diverse achievement. Caravaggio's influence was hardly established by the date of ter Brugghen's return north and so he must have derived this influence from the other Utrecht painters returning from Italy, such as Baburen and Honthorst. Ter Brugghen's dark pictures are in any case based on direct observation of the fall of artificial light rather than on second-hand sources. However, it was ter Brugghen's reliance on other sources which produced some of his most spectacular and moving pictures, such as *The Crucifixion* (New York, Metropolitan Museum), which is based on Dürer. Towards the end of the 1620s ter Brugghen's palette grew lighter (as did that of Honthorst) but he never came under the spell of the newly fashionable classicism as did van Bijlert and Honthorst. In his turn ter Brugghen was influential on the early work of Vermeer of Delft and especially on Vermeer's *Christ in the House of Martha and Mary* (Edinburgh, National Gallery).

8. A laughing Bravo, 1625
canvas; 104.8 × 85.1 cm
Royal Collection, Hampton Court
Reproduced by gracious permission of Her Majesty The Queen
One of the contradictions and great merits of ter Brugghen's art is his ability to paint vulgar subjects with a perfection of tone and colour, an achievement repeated by the young Vermeer of Delft, whose ambitious *Procuress* (Dresden, Gemäldegalerie) does precisely this. In this instance the whole surface is treated as if it were an exquisite still-life even though there is anything but cool calm detachment in the figure himself. Such subject-matter was very popular in Italy, especially among Caravaggio's followers, and ter Brugghen is continuing an Italian tradition rather than a northern one. The chromatic intensity of the drapery is another of ter Brugghen's hallmarks and this too may well be derived from Italian Mannerist painters such as Pontormo and Rosso, who employed such colours with dramatic effect. To paint a 'bravo' as an independent subject rather than as part of a moral or religious story reveals a new sophistication in the North.

8

Mathias Stomer

Amersfoort ?date unknown – Sicily after 1650

Although traditionally a native of Amersfoort, all Stomer's documented career was spent in Italy, firstly in Rome in the early 1630s and later in Naples and from 1641 onwards in Sicily. Stomer's art is unique among his Dutch contemporaries. His style was formed under the influence of Caravaggio, but did not thereafter change as did that of other painters, Dutch and Italian. Almost all Stomer's works are artificially lit (usually by candles) and his models are usually rustic, who often feature in *Adoration(s) of the Shepherds.* Although in his last years in Sicily he would have known the late work of Caravaggio, Stomer was unaffected by Caravaggio's sense of pathos and drama.

9. An old Woman and a Boy by Candlelight
panel; 48.4 × 71.1 cm
Birmingham City Museums and Art Gallery

This is one of Stomer's relatively rare genre scenes; he generally preferred much more elaborate religious and history subjects. The theme of a single person or couple seen by candlelight was a popular one in the period, especially with the northern followers of Caravaggio even though Caravaggio did not originate the type himself. In fact there are precedents in the work of El Greco rather than in Italian art. The caprice of shielding the candle flame with the hand was also favoured by contemporaries such as Georges de La Tour, although Stomer is unlikely to have been familiar with his work. The picture does not have to be read other than as a piece of simple genre through which the artist delights in facial expression and the fall of light.

9 [colour plate III]

Jan van Bijlert

Utrecht 1598 – Utrecht 1671

Bijlert is the least known of the so-called Utrecht Caravaggesques and was the least indebted to Caravaggio. He spent a short time in Rome (1621-23) and there came into contact with the work of his Utrecht contemporaries, especially Baburen and Honthorst, and on his return Bijlert painted a few overtly Caravaggesque pictures such as the *St Sebastian* of 1624 (Rohrau, Austria, Harrach Collection). He soon abandoned this severe manner for the bland classicism he was to follow for most of the rest of his career. This abrupt change was almost certainly instituted by Honthorst around 1625, who adopted a lighter and more classically inspired style which was at once *internationally* fashionable. Ter Brugghen lightened his palette in the mid-1620s and Bijlert, the least inventive of the Utrecht group, followed suit. At the end of his long career Bijlert's pictures had lost all their Italianate flavour and resembled local genre pieces (*eg* the paintings in the Bowes Museum, Barnard Castle).

10

10. Granida and Daifilo

canvas; 96.5 × 137.2 cm

Towneley Hall Art Gallery and Museum, Burnley Borough Council

The play *Granida and Daifilo* by Pieter Cornelis Hooft was very popular in the 1620s and both Honthorst (Utrecht, Centraal Museum) and Baburen (Brussels, Musées Royaux des Beaux-Arts) painted subjects from it. The story is about the romantic attraction of Granida, the daughter of the king of Persia, for the shepherd Daifilo. After various adventures they find true love and live happily ever after. This interpretation by Bijlert does not seem to reflect any particular moment in the story as do the pictures by Honthorst and Baburen, but concentrates on the romantic attraction of characters who are socially ill-matched. Such an interpretation of the subject has provided the artist with an excuse for a picture of sexual innuendo. Daifilo invites the spectator to share his lascivious thoughts for the sleeping Granida whose rank is indicated, even in a state of undress, by her jewellery. The essence of Hooft's play is the idyll of pastoral existence which frequently appears in Dutch 17th-century painting, portraits as well as landscapes.

On grounds of style it is likely that this picture was painted in the late 1620s, as from 1630 onwards Bijlert's style became much blander and less obviously derived from that of Honthorst. The history of this previously unpublished picture is unknown before it reached the Padiham Museum, from which it has been transferred in recent years to the Towneley Hall Museum.

Hendrick Bloemaert

Utrecht *c.*1609 – Utrecht 1672

Hendrick Bloemaert was the son and pupil of Abraham Bloemaert and imitated his father's style. He made a few concessions to changed times in the middle years of the century by introducing some of the bland classicising flavour fashionable both in Utrecht and Haarlem from the mid-1620s. It is surprising how both he and his father could continue successful careers despite changes in fashion.

11. St John the Baptist, 1624
canvas; 81.2 × 66.3 cm
Glasgow Museums and Art Galleries
This painting is a good example of a picture which would be acceptable to a Dutch Catholic. The Baptist is shown with attributes from Catholic iconography such as the cross and lamb symbolising Christ and the Crucifixion. Parts of the picture, *eg* the foreground vegetation, are realistically observed, while others, such as the leaves in the upper left corners, still betray Mannerist conventions. The treatment of the figure is up-to-date in the sense that the style is more classicising than Mannerist and described without sharp contrasts of tone or colour.

11

Cornelis van Poelenburgh

Utrecht *c.*1594/95 – Utrecht 1667

Poelenburgh's long career was especially influential in the field of Italianate landscape painting and in his lifetime he was one of the most international of Dutch painters. His style developed little after he had achieved a precocious maturity in his early years in Rome. He specialised in small-scale landscapes, usually containing figures bathing and, more rarely, in religious subjects. The lighting in these pictures is consistently Italian. Unlike most of his Dutch contemporaries in Italy, Poelenburgh achieved a considerable degree of official patronage, notably from the Grand Duke of Tuscany in Florence (a number of his pictures remain in the Galleria Pitti there). He was back in Utrecht in 1627 where he remained for most of the rest of his life. He was summoned to England by Charles I in 1637, presumably to execute a number of landscapes for the Royal Collection. Poelenburgh almost never dated his pictures and they remain difficult to date because of the consistency of his style with the exception of a few early attempts at painting topographical landscapes in Rome. Poelenburgh's art was much imitated by followers and pupils towards the end of the century, especially in The Hague and Utrecht, *eg* by Johan van Haensbergen, Dirck van der Lisse and Daniel Vertangen.

12

12. Landscape with Figures
canvas; 29.2 × 36.8 cm
Trustees of the Holburne Museum, Bath

This is a typical example of Poelenburgh's mature style and probably painted in Utrecht rather than in Italy. All the familiar elements are present, from the golden glow in the sky to the figures both clothed and naked among picturesque classical ruins. Such pictures conjured up nostalgia for a classical antiquity familiar to most educated Dutchmen. Unlike those of most of his contemporaries, Poelenburgh's pictures are vaguely *poetical* in intent like those of Claude Lorrain in Rome. Poelenburgh was apparently uninterested in exploring the possibilities of Dutch landscape or experimenting with atmosphere and composition like Dujardin and Lingelbach, Italianate landscapists of the next generation.

Jan Both

Utrecht *c.*1618 – Utrecht 1652

In the context of Dutch Italianate landscape painting Jan Both made an important contribution because he imported a certain type of composition and atmosphere which was to influence the course of Dutch landscape painting for the rest of the century. This contribution was dependent on achievements of artists working in Italy, especially of Claude. This closeness to Claude made Jan Both, in the early years of the 19th century, the most expensive and sought-after of all Dutch landscapists. His reputation declined from the mid-19th century onwards due to the increasingly nationalistic approach of Italian and Dutch art historians. Jan Both can be appreciated today as one of the finest landscape painters of his time, understanding and describing the fall of light better than Berchem, for instance, who sometimes imitated him in composition.

13. Italian Landscape with Muleteers
canvas; 126 × 160 cm
The Visitors of the Ashmolean Museum, Oxford
At first sight this landscape appears contrived. Such pictures were created to a specific formula but that formula was based on a careful observation of the hilly countryside around Rome. Many of the Dutch artists working in Rome went out into the countryside to make sketches of ruins and trees which they could then include in their idyllic landscapes. Both captures the golden glow of the Roman Campagna rather than the light of Northern Europe and introduces a further reference to Italy through the muleteers. It is likely that most of Jan Both's pictures of this type were, however, executed after he had left Italy and returned to Utrecht.

13

14 [colour plate XVIII]

Jan Weenix

Amsterdam 1642? – Amsterdam 1719

He was the pupil of his short-lived father, Jan Baptist Weenix, who specialised in Italianate scenes with ports, harbours and figures. He abandoned his father's style soon after the latter's death in the early 1660s and spent the rest of his long career preoccupied with dead game. Most of these pictures are remarkably skilled in their depiction of fur, weapons and feathers and they are inventive in their composition. This genre is not currently fashionable and, therefore, Weenix's reputation is at a relatively low ebb even though he brought the Dutch game piece to its highest point.

15

14. Landscape with a Shepherd Boy, 1664
canvas; 81.6 × 99.6 cm
Reproduced by permission of the Governors of Dulwich Picture Gallery
This is one of the rare pictures by Jan Weenix painted under the direct influence of his father, Jan Baptist Weenix, and it is one of his best works painted with great freedom of brush-work and liveliness of observation. It is not known whether the artist visited Italy but he manages the conventions with adequate skill. The scene is in the Campagna littered with ruins from classical antiquity. A shepherd boy is removing fleas from his dog as the other dog in characteristic pose looks on. There is the feeling in this picture that the whole is observed as an actual incident rather than as a repeated convention. The sheep are well drawn and anticipate the artist's later preoccupation with animals, mostly dead.

Jacob de Heusch
Utrecht 1657 – Amsterdam 1701

Jacob de Heusch was the nephew of Willem de Heusch, a follower of Jan Both. Much of his career was spent in Italy where he specialised in landscape. Almost all his pictures betray the influence of Salvator Rosa both in composition and colour. As a result of his effective Italianism, de Heusch has been neglected by historians of Dutch painting, unlike a number of his Italianate Dutch contemporaries such as Hoet (p.71) whose Italianate landscapes are close in mood to those of the French artist (resident in Rome) Gaspard Dughet.

15. Classical Landscape with Figures
canvas; 88.2 × 130.2 cm
Herbert Art Gallery, Coventry
Almost every element in this broad composition is derived from the work of Salvator Rosa although each is given a rather lighter and more refined treatment; de Heusch was never able to capture the melancholy and drama of Salvator's landscapes. The landscape is fanciful and not based on an accurate observation of a specific scene. This is in contrast to the earlier generation of Dutch Italianate landscapists who achieve a strong sense of place even when not attempting topographical accuracy.

Middelburg

As part of the Province of Zeeland, Middelburg joined the Union of Utrecht in 1579. However, Zeeland never enjoyed the mercantile prosperity enjoyed by Holland which lay to the north. Apart from the main port of Flushing (Vlissingen), Middelburg was the only town of consequence. It had been laid out in the 15th century and did not greatly change during the 17th century. Its elaborate late-medieval buildings can be seen in the early paintings of Adriaen van de Venne but no topographer of note records the appearance of Middelburg later on although Jan van der Heyden, an Amsterdam artist, made views of the small Zeeland town of Veere which by then was also in decline.

Given the relatively simple rural and seafaring economy of Middelburg, it is surprising that so many painters of consequence worked in the city at various times throughout the century. They never formed a school like those of Leiden, Haarlem, Delft or Utrecht but nevertheless had more identifiable character than can be found in remoter provinces, such as Groningen, where only a few portraitists were active.

Of all the main Dutch centres of population, Middelburg was the closest to Antwerp which remained the richest city in the whole of the Netherlands, north and south, until *c.*1640 when the effects of the Dutch blockade began to be felt. The arrival of Antwerp-born painters such as Ambrosius Bosschaert, a specialist flower painter, gave Middelburg early artistic pre-eminence. A recent exhibition held at the Waterman Gallery, Amsterdam ('The flower lovers of Middelburg') demonstrated the extent of Middelburg's fondness for flower drawings, paintings and illustrations in the 1620s and 1630s. Another immigrant from Antwerp was the eccentric and often mysterious Adriaen van de Venne who spent the first half of his career in Middelburg and brought with him a Brueghel-inspired sense of peasant humour and occasional pathos.

The principal artists active in Middelburg during the middle years of the century were Dirck van Delen (p.53) and Daniel de Blieck (p.54) and towards the end of the period the still shadowy figure of Adriaen Coorte (p.55) who worked for some twenty years in the town. With the meticulous art of Coorte the stylistic cycle came full circle and his attention to detail and clarity of expression marks a return to the ideals of Ambrosius Bosschaert. Generally, the second half of the century did not fulfil earlier promise and this no doubt reflected the fact that, in comparison with other major centres, Middelburg was then in economic decline.

16

Adriaen Pietersz. van de Venne
Delft 1589 – The Hague 1662

Adriaen van de Venne is a complex artist whose achievements have yet to be properly understood. His conventional works were small winter scenes or other seasons painted in a Flemish manner. Otherwise he devoted most of his long career to a series of peasant scenes illustrating Dutch proverbs. Some of these bear inscriptions which make the moral clear. Many more, however, are uninscribed, probably because the particular moral would have been obvious at the time. Van de Venne should be valued for not making poverty picturesque but for showing it as distressing, mocking, cruel and ugly. This honesty has cost him popular estimation.

16. A Scene of Witchcraft
canvas; 23.8 × 36.1 cm
Nottingham Castle Museum and Art Gallery
Adriaen van de Venne's curious and personal technique contrasts with the more usual Dutch preoccupation with perfect surface texture. Van de Venne's technique is appropriate to the mood of horror that he sought to express. The figures are fleeing from some unseen source of fear – it may be that a figure of death is to be imagined. The figure of grotesque terror on the extreme left anticipates a modern approach to such images. It is not clear whether this picture illustrates a particular proverb (most proverb pictures are neatly inscribed in Gothic letters) or whether this is just a piece of painful reality. It cannot be over-emphasised that most Dutch artists show the poorer classes in an edited and prettified form for the appreciation of the better-off. The poor did not own the pictures in which they so often featured.

17

Dirck van Delen
Heusden 1605 – Arnemuiden 1671

Even though he worked in the relative isolation of Arnemuiden near Middelburg, van Delen's pictures usually have the cosmopolitan feel of a large centre. This resulted from the strong Antwerp influence on his general treatment of the subject and the fact that he consistently used other artists, such as Jan Olis and Anthonie Palamedes, for his figures. Most of van Delen's pictures are of courtyards or gardens of imaginary palaces typical of Antwerp rather than of cities in the Dutch Republic. Delen also painted a memorable still-life of a tulip in a vase (Rotterdam, Boymans–van Beuningen Museum).

17. A Game of Skittles in a Garden, 1636
panel; 67.3 × 82.3 cm
Shipley Art Gallery, Gateshead (Tyne and Wear Museums Service)
This picture is entirely typical of van Delen's style as is that of the animated figures added by a collaborator, almost certainly in this instance Anthonie Palamedes. The architecture and garden ornaments are fanciful and create a mood of arcadian opulence. There are, however, a few realistic touches which are worth noting – the layout of the garden in formal parterres with attendant gardeners and the tulips planted in serried ranks. *Informality* in nature is an entirely 18th-century concept and in the 17th century all gardening was strictly formal and symmetrical.

18

Daniel de Blieck
?*c.*1630 – Middelburg 1673

Few details are known of de Blieck's career but he seems to have worked in Middelburg for most of his life. However, his most often repeated subject is the spacious Gothic interior of the church of St Laurens at Rotterdam. De Blieck's church interiors follow conventions invented by Houckgeest – that of spacious perspectives and light colours, but de Blieck gives them his own personal flavour through a more relaxed treatment of the individual forms. Almost all the great Dutch church interior painters, especially Saenredam, achieve their ends by a taut precision based on meticulous site drawing. De Blieck, on the other hand, probably relied much more on a formula.

18. Alexander the Great slaying his General Cleitus, 1663
canvas; 113.7 × 126.4 cm
Ferens Art Gallery : Hull City Museums and Art Galleries
This dramatic picture is unusual for de Blieck as most of his few surviving works are church interiors. The fashion for painting Baroque interiors of this type appeared in Dutch

painting in the 1660s. Emanuel de Witte painted a few church interiors in this manner as did Rutger van Langeveldt (example at Gateshead). Here grand Baroque architecture serves as a setting for Alexander the Great's brutal murder of his general Cleitus who had saved his life at the Battle of Granicus. The likely moral meaning has not been interpreted.

Adriaen Coorte

working Middelburg 1685-1707

Coorte remains one of the least documented of all Dutch 17th-century painters. Most of his dated pictures come from the last decade of the century and there is evidence that he worked in Middelburg at a time when there were few other painters active there. All but a handful of his pictures concentrate on still-life with remarkably few elements – a bunch of asparagus, a few gooseberries, a few sea shells. The utter simplicity of these pictures gives them a timeless quality which does not immediately identify them with the 17th-century Dutch tradition. Coorte painted a few rather more elaborate pictures such as the *Exotic Birds* (see below).

19. Exotic Birds, 1683
canvas; 39 × 48 cm
The Visitors of the Ashmolean Museum, Oxford
Birds are common enough in Dutch 17th-century painting and there were several specialists in this genre, the best known being Melchior d'Hondecoeter. When the fastidious Coorte turned to this well-established genre the result was surprising. The ridiculous shape of the large pelican is emphasised by its isolation in the composition. The ducks on the right are relatively animated. Further anecdote is provided by the duck and the frog staring each other out; the gull with its bill open seems indifferent to the creatures near it. The picture is the artist's earliest dated work and the only one of this type to have survived. It seems quite likely that there are more to be discovered but if unsigned they would be difficult indeed to attribute.

19

Leiden

Until overtaken by Amsterdam at the end of the first quarter of the 17th century, Leiden was the most populous city of the Northern Netherlands. It became the seat of the leading university of the time and until the middle years of the century the richness and variety of its artistic life was comparable to that of Utrecht, Haarlem and Amsterdam. Artistic activity declined from about 1660.

With Utrecht, Leiden played a leading role in late-medieval and early-Renaissance painting, the chief figure being Lucas van Leyden. Almost all the major achievements of this period were destroyed, however, in the iconoclastic crisis and van Leyden's *Last Judgement* altarpiece alone remains in the town (Stedelijk Museum 'De Lakenhal').

Leiden's importance as a city and the fact that it had a long painting tradition would lead one to expect artistic continuity in the 17th century. In fact the stylistic homogeneity of Leiden art is remarkable and gave rise to the term the *Leiden* school of 'fijnschilders'. The evolution of this school was chiefly inspired by three painters who collaborated with and were influenced by each other: Gerrit Dou (p.60), Jan Lievens (p.58) and Rembrandt. All three painters came from different stylistic starting points but in the late 1620s reacted to each other so strongly that there was, in microcosm, the genesis of a great school of painting. Dou, always meticulous, came under the young Rembrandt's spell and then remained in Leiden painting ever more detailed but sombre pictures. He had a number of pupils including Frans van Mieris the Elder. Jan Lievens, on the other hand, came closer to Rembrandt in mood but not in style creating a few individual masterpieces such as the Brighton *Raising of Lazarus* (p.58). After leaving Leiden, Lievens did not live up to his early promise and too easily adopted current fashions, being influenced by Anthony van Dyck among others. Rembrandt, though in Leiden for only a very few years before his departure at the end of 1631, painted a large number of highly skilled pictures for which, even if he had died at twenty-five, he would still be given an honourable place in the history of Dutch painting. Almost all Rembrandt's Leiden pictures are small in scale and not one of them gives any indication of the artist's precocious achievement from the moment that he arrived in Amsterdam, signalled by his first major picture, *The Anatomy Lesson of Dr Tulp* (The Hague, Mauritshuis).

The very unity of the Leiden genre painters and the continuation of the tradition to the middle years of the 18th century, has sometimes led to the neglect of the other types of painting practised in Leiden such as Rembrandt's cabinet pieces of the 1620s. Almost all the Leiden genre painters produced small-scale pictures and this is a marked feature of Leiden paintings as a whole. It is curious that Leiden painters should have avoided bright or even saturated colour and this may be due to the influence of Dou. Other painters too, such as Jan Porcellis (p.58), employed the same palette for seascape painting in parallel with van Goyen's landscape and river scenes (p.60).

Topographically Leiden lacked the interest of many other centres and few painters were attracted to the barn-like silhouettes of its two towerless medieval churches. Even canal scenes are rare.

Looked at from a 17th-century point of view, Leiden was at the very centre of Dutch painting despite the fact that by modern reckoning not a single truly great painter worked there with the exception of Rembrandt in his early years. Gerrit Dou was the highest-paid Dutch painter of his time and Leiden school pictures were avidly sought after by collectors from all over Europe (hence the conspicuous lack of them today in the Stedelijk Museum 'De Lakenhal', Leiden).

Leiden school

20. Portrait of Nicolaes Warmondt of Leiden, 1607
panel; 109 × 76.2 cm
Royal Albert Memorial Museum, Exeter
The sitter is identifiable both from a contemporary inscription on the back (which is rare) and from a portrait of the same sitter twenty years earlier (Stedelijk Museum 'De Lakenhal', Leiden). Official portraiture had reached a high level by 1600 in the wealthier Dutch towns and cities, although relatively little of this seems to have survived. The few group portraits by Cornelis van Haarlem and the portraits by Wttewael, neither of whom is known for portraiture, is evidence for this. The treatment of this burgomaster portrait, taken at the end of his life (he died in 1608), seems conventional enough even to the inclusion of a Vanitas motif with the hand on the skull. What gives this otherwise conventional picture some importance is the fact that it is very similar to a portrait of a few years later by the young Frans Hals – an *Unidentified Man with a Skull* (Birmingham, Barber Institute).

20

Jan Porcellis

Ghent 1587 – Zoeterwoude 1632

Porcellis was one of the most important contributors to the early development of seascape painting in the Dutch Republic. He did not follow the tradition established in Haarlem by the Vrooms, father and son, but went his own way observing the austerity and greyness of the North Sea and the estuaries which opened out into it. He did not delight in the complexity of ship's rigging nor was he interested in painting ship's portraits, as was fashionable later in the century. His art inspired Simon de Vlieger who developed a powerful monochrome style in the 1630s and 1640s. Porcellis' work is rare as he died young.

21

21. Mussel Fishing
canvas; 51 × 63.5 cm
National Maritime Museum
Fishing scenes are curiously rare in Dutch seascape painting, the preference being for dramatic storms, sea battles or accurate portraits of ships. The humble act of fishing, an everyday necessity in the long Dutch winters in order to feed the city populations, seems to have attracted very little attention among the seascape specialists although fishermen are often shown by Jan van Goyen. In this picture Porcellis has employed his usual simplicity of composition and restraint with colour.

Jan Lievens

Leiden 1607 – Amsterdam 1674

The career of Jan Lievens has been neglected until recent years. He has always been overshadowed by his contemporary and collaborator in his early years in Leiden, Rembrandt. Lievens' later work has been neglected because it became so internationally eclectic. He began precociously in Leiden, having been taught by Lastman in Amsterdam (like Rembrandt) and in the late 1620s Lievens and Rembrandt were extremely close and even shared a studio. When Rembrandt left Leiden for Amsterdam at the end of 1631 never to return, Lievens changed direction and for the rest of his long career came under a variety of influences which make his art difficult to characterise and his real achievement difficult to assess. The pictures which are close to Rembrandt have always been the ones most esteemed and studied (see *The Raising of Lazarus* below). In the early 1630s he is said to have visited England and certainly spent some years in Antwerp where his style was profoundly influenced by Anthony van Dyck's portraits which were fashionable there. Later in his career he had official patronage from Amalia von Solms (as did Rembrandt) but his later pictures never lived up to the promise of his earlier years with the exception of a small group of mysterious landscapes which are totally original. In their shadowed density they appear superficially Rembrandtesque but they owe nothing to Rembrandt's own landscape style.

22. The Raising of Lazarus
canvas; 106.8 × 114.3 cm
The Royal Pavilion, Art Gallery and Museums, Brighton
This picture, Lievens' masterpiece, is for several reasons a work of great importance. The fact that it almost certainly belonged to Rembrandt gives it a *cachet* unusual enough as so few Dutch artists can be proved to have collected the work of their contemporaries. From the stylistic point of view the importance of the picture has been much discussed although the conclusions which can be drawn from the evidence are ambiguous.

The facts are simple enough – Rembrandt made a painting of the same subject (Los Angeles County Museum) which has always been dated to *c.* 1630 and, therefore, it has always been concluded that Lievens based himself on the Rembrandt, which in itself is an innovative and bold composition breaking new ground in Rembrandt's rapid development around 1630. If the dating of the Los Angeles Rembrandt is correct, then Lievens would have *developed* Rembrandt's composition into something even bolder and more original. On the other hand, the evidence suggests that it may have been Rembrandt who derived his own picture from knowledge of the Lievens; the date of Rembrandt's picture only has to be moved forward one year for this to be hypothetically possible. The fact remains, however, that the Lievens composition is the more

22

original and has several characteristics which make it unique in the context of its time. A recently-taken X-ray of the painting has revealed traces of a figure (?portrait) subject beneath the *Raising of Lazarus* thus adding a further question about the genesis of this work.

Lazarus is represented merely by two shadowy hands rising from the tomb, the eye being drawn up by the curve of the winding sheet. The exaggerated poses of the figures and their faces express *trauma* in a way not repeated before Fuseli in the late-18th century. Such an emotional approach was only otherwise achieved by Rembrandt many years later. It appears, therefore, that Lievens led the way in this eccentric picture reminding us that in the history of painting advances are not made slowly and logically but by sudden leaps not always apparent to the artist's contemporaries. In this case Lievens' masterpiece found an admirer in Rembrandt himself.

Jan van Goyen

Leiden 1596 – The Hague 1656

Along with Jacob van Ruisdael, Meindert Hobbema and Aelbert Cuyp, Jan van Goyen is now regarded as one of the leading Dutch landscapists of the 17th century. This has not always been so because from the end of the 17th century to the end of the 19th his freedom of brushwork or 'Impressionism' was totally out of fashion with connoisseurs of *Dutch* painting. Jan van Goyen's career, although peripatetic (he lived in Haarlem, Leiden and The Hague and evidently visited most towns and villages in the Dutch Republic or just over the German border), falls into clear categories. At the start he was very much under the influence of Esaias van de Velde whom he had known in Haarlem and whose precise colouring, clear horizons, brightly-coloured figures and an overall restless effect he adopted. Around 1630 van Goyen muted his palette and increased the freedom of his brushwork. For the rest of his career the changes were more subtle with occasional referrals to his previous style. Later in the 1630s, for instance, the artist began to reintroduce colour into some of his pictures, introducing patches of blue in an otherwise grey sky and a slight pinkishness to the horizon. During this period his brushwork was becoming looser while all other Dutch painters became more precise and detailed. Any explanation of this phenomenon in van Goyen's art can only be hypothetical. There is evidence to show that the artist had financial difficulties, through speculation in tulip bulbs, and this may have led him to increase output at the expense of detail. Alternatively he was aiming at atmospheric effect. Whatever the reason, van Goyen remains one of the great individual spirits of Dutch 17th-century painting.

23. River Scene, 1642
canvas; 97.8 × 131.4 cm
Birmingham City Museums and Art Gallery
In scale and achievement this is one of van Goyen's most successful river scenes. The artist's preoccupation is with the effects of weather. The skill of later artists in conveying cloud effects and the feeling of moisture in the air has obscured Jan van Goyen's innovatory role and influence. The sky, which forms two-thirds of the picture, is the direct ancestor of Constable's cloud studies. Constable disliked the Dutch Italianates, especially Berchem, for setting a bad example to his contemporaries who looked at art rather than nature. The exact site from which this picture was taken has not been identified. It is likely to be one of the distributaries of the Rhine, such as the Merwede which flowed past Dordrecht. (The present configuration of the waterways and coast has been radically altered since the 17th century.)

23 [colour plate V]

Gerrit Dou
Leiden 1613 – Leiden 1675

Dou was the most important painter of the Leiden school and the founder of a style which became known as the Leiden 'fijnschilders' (literally fine painters). He began as a pupil and collaborator of Rembrandt in Leiden in the 1620s and it seems that Dou was much more skilled than Rembrandt in creating detailed effects, but had no interest in expressing human emotions or the complex relationships necessary to successful Bible illustration. As soon as Rembrandt left Leiden permanently at the end of 1631 and set up in Amsterdam, Dou was on his own and became cocooned in a repetitive approach for forty years. His pictures are rarely larger than six or seven inches square, with only two or three figures. Subject-matter is restricted to a narrow range. We may well ask why such modesty of scale, subject-matter and lack of innovation should allow Dou such importance in the development of a whole school of painting. Dou's skilful handling of incredible amounts of detail without spoiling the unity of the composition and his ability to be varied within narrowly defined limits enabled him to be a source of inspiration to a whole generation of painters (*eg* Frans van Mieris (p.62), Dominicus van Tol (p.64), Gabriel Metsu (p.61)) and this influence lasted until the Leiden school petered out towards the end of the 18th century.

24. The Onion Chopper, 1646
panel; 18 × 14.8 cm
Royal Collection, London
Reproduced by gracious permission of Her Majesty The Queen

24 [colour plate XII]

25 [colour plate VIII]

The minute scale of this picture makes it difficult to appreciate outside the context of individual contemplation. Such pictures were kept in small rooms and often had little curtains protecting them (*trompe l'œil* curtains are sometimes included in a painting). Unusual in a genre painting is the onion chopper's outward look at the spectator. This is rare in Dutch genre painting although it occurs in some of Vermeer's Delft interiors. In the precision of this tiny piece there is not the slightest indication of the influence of Rembrandt.

Gabriel Metsu

Leiden 1629 – Amsterdam 1667

Metsu was one of the most important of all Dutch painters of pure genre, although he was perhaps one of the least influential. He was inventive within a very narrow range. After a few religious pieces and low-life genre, he settled down to paint a relatively modest number of small-scale and highly finished works. The best known of these is *The Music Lesson* in the National Gallery, London. As a moralist and an observer of the human condition he stands midway between those artists who always pointed to an obvious moral (Rembrandt) and those who generally avoided it (Pieter de Hooch). In spite of his preoccupation with silks and satins Metsu was able to depict character extremely well, even if he did not always exploit the complex relationships between the characters in his pictures.

25. The Cello Player
canvas; 62.8 × 47.6 cm
Royal Collection, London
Reproduced by gracious permission of Her Majesty The Queen
The precise event taking place in this picture has never been satisfactorily explained. The lady appears to be showing the cello player a large piece of paper, although it could well be a sheet of music rather than a letter. The spectator on the upper level has a weary expression as if he knows exactly what is happening between the two main characters. This ambiguity of meaning is almost certainly deliberate allowing the onlooker to speculate. The picture is painted with Metsu's characteristic skill but on a slightly larger scale than is usual for him.

Frans van Mieris I

Leiden 1635 – Leiden 1681

Frans van Mieris was the leading pupil of Gerrit Dou in Leiden and himself fathered a tradition which lasted until the mid-18th century owing to the fact that his son, pupil and imitator, Willem van Mieris, lived on until that date. Van Mieris altered Dou's rather shadowy style into something brighter and clearer but equally detailed and small-scale. He painted rather similar subjects, mostly genre pieces and occasionally small portraits which almost qualify as miniatures. Van Mieris' technique is, if anything, even more miraculous than that of Dou as the illusion of three dimensions could be depicted in a very small space and, unlike the work of Dou, could still be seen at a reasonable distance. Van Mieris was immensely successful in his lifetime achieving an international reputation.

Attributed to Frans van Mieris
26. A Music Party
panel; 34.2 × 28.8 cm
Bristol City Art Gallery
There is some dispute about the attribution of this picture and the van Mieris signature may be false, but this is nevertheless a good example of a Leiden genre piece. All the familiar elements are there – the music-making, the elaborate carpet on the table and the ostentatious display of skill in the painting of the cello leaning against the box on the right. The treatment of the subject implies a date later than *c.*1670 as there is a subtlety and wistfulness which was not part of the earlier genre pieces. The violin player is lost in a reverie while the two figures at the table concentrate on each other. It is possible that this picture is an early work by Willem van Mieris at the time when he was imitating the work of his father.

26

Jan Steen

Leiden 1626 – Leiden 1679

In terms of subject-matter and its interpretation Jan Steen is one of the most complex of all Dutch 17th-century painters. He is perhaps best known as the painter of domestic disorder (the Dutch now describe domestic chaos as a 'Jan Steen household') but his subject-matter is much more varied as he painted bourgeois genre scenes as well as a good number of religious and historical pictures. His style was very uneven in quality ranging from the highly finished to the sketchy and could be downright shoddy on occasion. In spite of this unevenness of execution his powers of observation and satire never left him. Almost all his pictures expose human foibles, sometimes in a humorous way but more often with biting wit. The artist's stylistic development is rather difficult to follow as he seems to have used his rough and smooth techniques in parallel. In general, as he grew older, the meticulously finished pictures grew fewer.

27. The Physician visiting a sick Girl
canvas; 71.1 × 57.2 cm
University of Edinburgh (Torrie Collection)
As is usual with Jan Steen this picture is not an accurate record of the ministrations of the medical profession but an attack on hypochondria and medical greed. The affluent-looking doctor is accepting, with mock humility, a glass of good wine from the knowing maidservant. The patient appears to be in the throes of a serious fever until we realise that she is sick with love. Her lover waits outside and can just be seen through the window in the background. The moral is made more obvious by the picture on the wall which probably depicts the tragic story of Venus and Adonis. Another version (The Hague, Mauritshuis) is given a slightly different slant by the omission of the waiting man and the inclusion of a much more explicit picture on the wall – *The Abduction of Hippodamia*. The Hague picture is generally dated *c.*1660 and this picture is likely to come from the same time, *ie* just after the artist had left Delft.

27

28

Dominicus van Tol

Bodegraven *c.*1635 – Leiden 1676

Dominicus van Tol was a minor painter but in the variety of his subjects and treatment of detail epitomises the Leiden school at its peak in the middle years of the century. Almost all the great Leiden painters, in particular Dou and Frans van Mieris the Elder, were specialists and changed relatively little in style or subject-matter. Van Tol, on the other hand, could adopt the style and composition of almost all his contemporaries, only giving himself away by the fact that his figures and details are rather less refined and consequently took less time to execute. There is no public collection where a selection of his work can be seen and his paintings are widely scattered.

28. A Lady at the Virginals
panel; 33 × 27.3 cm
Essex County Council, Chelmsford Shire Hall
The theme of well-dressed ladies playing the virginals was commonly treated by Dutch 17th-century painters, for example by Ochtervelt (p.116) and Vermeer of Delft (p.108), and it was especially popular with Leiden painters, Dou and Metsu in particular. In this picture the carpet and figure are carefully painted but the elaborate hangings in the background are much more sketchily indicated. The facial type is characteristic of van Tol and emphasises the repetitive nature of the artist's work.

Jacob Toorenvliet

Leiden 1640 – Leiden 1719

Toorenvliet was one of the last exponents of the Leiden school of genre painting outside the influence of the van Mieris dynasty which dominated painting in the city until the middle of the 18th century. Toorenvliet had no particular style of his own. In his low-life scenes there are reminiscences of Jan Steen (*The Couple* in the Stedelijk Museum 'De Lakenhal', Leiden, even bears a false Jan Steen signature). In his middle-class genre pictures Frans van Mieris had some effect on him yet in general atmosphere the chief influence is the early work of Metsu, especially such pictures as the *Couple at Wine* (Cheltenham Art Gallery). Toorenvliet painted an unusually wide range of genre, not limiting himself to one social class.

29. The Dentist
metal; 31.8 × 24.7 cm
The Royal Pavilion, Art Gallery and Museums, Brighton
The main influence in this dramatic little picture is Jan Steen and even the facial type of the dentist is derived from him. As with medical pictures of the time there is an element of fun or mockery; the dentist is a quack who resorts to superstition as indicated by the skull on the barrel. This is in direct contrast to the real and earnest sense of medical enquiry which preoccupied the Dutch and which is illustrated in pictures of anatomy lessons. Toorenvliet's career cannot be defined and it is not clear whether he continued to paint low-life genre scenes towards the end of the century when, in general, they became less popular.

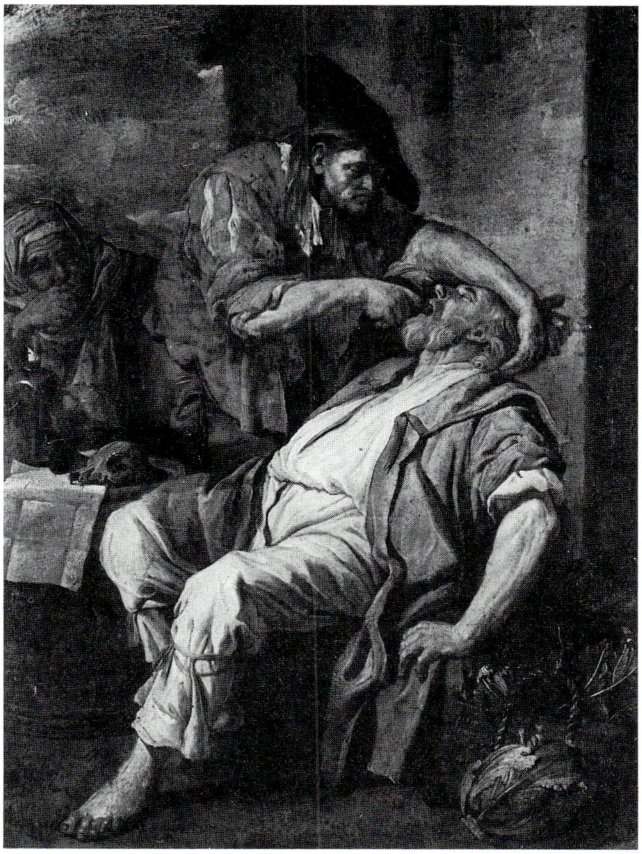

29

30

Abraham Jansz. Begijn
Leiden 1637/38 – Berlin 1697

Begijn belonged to no particular centre. His pictures are not as stylistically eclectic as might be expected for an artist born in Leiden, who trained in Haarlem, worked in Amsterdam and The Hague, visited Italy and ended his career in the employ of the Elector of Brandenburg (The Great Elector). His 'forest floor' landscapes, epitomised by Otto Marseus van Schrieck (p. 148), included well-painted animals comparable to those of the two Weenixes. Begijn's Italian port scenes were definitely influenced by Jan Baptist Weenix. However, Begijn's pictures are unmistakably his own and bear witness to direct study from nature rather than to second-hand observation alone.

30. Thistles with a Goat
canvas; 35.5 × 31.1 cm
Norfolk Museums Service (Norwich Castle Museum)
This splendid thistle is obviously drawn from nature as is the well-observed goat. Much less convincing is the tree in the background and the niche on the right betrays the artist's interest in Italianate landscapes. This type of picture has always been much more highly esteemed by the Dutch than by other collectors.

The Hague

The small town of The Hague assumed an importance throughout the 17th century out of all proportion to its size. This importance was entirely political and linked to its being the meeting place of The States General. The very modest extent of The Hague at this period can be appreciated even today and it would be entirely surprising if artistic activity had rivalled that of Delft only some five miles to the south. For most of the century there were only a limited number of painters active in the town and they were not connected to the Stadholders who, when the Orange family did undertake a rare major commission, sought artists from elsewhere. A *Passion Series* was commissioned from Rembrandt for instance (Munich, Alte Pinakothek) and the decoration of the Huis ten Bosch was mainly undertaken by Haarlem painters and the Flemish artist Jacob Jordaens. The limited patronage of the Stadholders had a stultifying effect on local painters because the population was not large enough to support the range of painters to be found in other centres. Those who were resident at The Hague had formed their styles elsewhere. Perhaps the most distinguished of them in the early part of the century was Esaias van de Velde.

A visible change took place in the last quarter of the century. This can be directly attributed to the increased status of the Stadholder. The French invasion of 1672 had established once and for all the primacy of the House of Orange over the Dutch State and from this point onwards it enjoyed the status of monarchy. The Revolution of 1688 in England brought the Stadholder Willem III to the English and Scottish thrones as William III.

A number of artists settled in The Hague and among them Ary de Vois from Utrecht. There grew up, almost overnight, a definable Hague school which is not usually recognised as such. All the painters concerned, de Vois, Schalcken, Netscher and Verelst, concentrated on a highly detached and sometimes dramatic approach. In scale and general tonality there is an influence of the Leiden 'fijnschilders' but a greater independence of spirit. This is characteristic of the work of Schalcken, who painted the Stadholder Willem III and was held in such high regard by him that he employed him in England too.

The congregation of so many relatively distinguished painters in The Hague during the final years of the century, gave to The Hague, together with Amsterdam, the last glow of the golden age.

31

Copy after ***Adriaen van de Venne***
(for biography see p.52)
31. The Dutch Princes out hunting
panel; 31.1 × 43.8 cm
Warwick District Council Museum Service, Leamington Spa Art Gallery
This picture is an old copy after an original van de Venne in the Hessisches Landesmuseum at Darmstadt. It shows Prince Maurits and his brothers out hunting near The Hague and even in such an 'official' piece the artist cannot resist including other events in the background. There are remarkably few such depictions of the hereditary ruling family of the Dutch Republic because in fact from the assassination of William the Silent in 1584 until the debacle of 1672 when the Stadholders resumed total power, the position of the Stadholder and his family was strictly limited within an oligarchical State. They never rivalled their Italian or French contemporaries as art patrons although from time to time they collected or commissioned significant works of art.

Anthony Jansz. van der Croos
(for biography see p.91)

32. Landscape with the Castle of Rijswijk
panel; 25.4 × 38.7 cm
Bowes Museum, Barnard Castle, Co. Durham
The important castle of Rijswijk stood just to the south of The Hague towards Delft and gave its name to the treaty of 1697 between Louis XIV of France and the Dutch, which ended a long period of struggle between the two countries. Nothing now remains of the substantial complex of buildings which, by Dutch standards, was palatial in scale. The view was a favourite of van der Croos, who was not very scrupulous about architectural detail. The style of the painting is comparable to a series of tiny topographical views dated 1665 (Toulouse, Musée des Augustins).

32

33 [colour plate XIX]

Joris van der Hagen
Arnhem or Dordrecht 1615 – The Hague 1669

Joris van der Hagen remains curiously little-known even though he was an accomplished landscape painter. He mastered both the Italianate landscape in the manner of Berchem as well as the realistic woodland landscape in the manner of Jacob van Ruisdael. His pictures have an added interest for showing the hilly landscape on the eastern borders of the Dutch Republic. The latter enabled him to use his skill for panorama – a difficult genre to master although easily taken for granted because of the achievement of Jacob van Ruisdael and Koninck. Van der Hagen was based in The Hague and became a member of the Guild there, but it is likely that he spent much of his time travelling to the sites he so often painted.

34

33. Landscape with a Castle
canvas; 94 × 118.2 cm
Derby Art Gallery
This dramatic landscape may represent the St Pieters Berg which is on a bluff near Maastricht. Rather similar topography appears in a picture with a much broader panorama in the Gemäldegalerie Schloss Wilhelmshöhe at Kassel. The artist reveals a strong debt to Jacob van Ruisdael, especially to the latter's views of the Castle of Bentheim set on the Dutch/German border. Recent cleaning has revealed great subtlety of tone and colour with a delicate harmony of the blues, browns and greens distinct from Ruisdael's bolder tones.

Ary de Vois
Utrecht 1631? – Leiden 1690

Ary de Vois' pictures vary in character, quality and subject-matter but they conform to the general taste of the last third of the century. His paintings are small in scale, minutely detailed and lacking obvious bravura of brushwork. Most of his career was spent in Utrecht although he died in The Hague. His style was formed as a pupil of a Leipzig-born painter working in

35

Utrecht, Nicolaes Knüpffer. His later style is a half-hearted response to current trends. De Vois painted small religious pictures in a manner favoured by Adriaen van der Werff and genre pieces more influenced by Schalcken, Netscher and Eglon van der Neer.

34. The Prodigal Son
panel; 22.8 × 18.3 cm
Trustees of the Holburne Museum, Bath
The Prodigal Son was a relevant story for a society so pre-occupied with material wealth. This is a moralising piece showing the prodigal son in a state of dissipation and consequent regret. Earlier in the century painters preferred to show him dissipating his patrimony, an excuse for a scene of revelry (*eg* a Cornelis van Haarlem in the Wadsworth Atheneum, Hartford, Connecticut).

Simon Verelst

The Hague 1644 – London 1721

Verelst is one of the few Dutch flower painters who worked for a good part of his career in England. Tradition has it that he claimed to be the God of Flowers. Although Verelst was bolder in composition, he was less skilled than Rachel Ruysch. Some of his pictures are characterised by a disarming simplicity – a good example being the *Daffodils in a Vase* (The Hague, Museum Bredius). Verelst also painted portraits, sometimes with flowers as a decorative adjunct thus advertising his talent (*eg* Barnsley, Cooper Art Gallery). The artist's style developed little and, therefore, his pictures are difficult to date.

35. Vase of Flowers
canvas; 51.4 × 50.6 cm
The Syndics of the Fitzwilliam Museum, Cambridge
This composition is unusually complex for Verelst who often preferred a simpler and less Baroque structure for his flower arrangements. Roses dominate and there are other summer flowers including a carnation and a poppy. Some of the flowers in this composition are wilting slightly and the leaves of the roses in the foreground have been partly eaten away by insects. In some contexts this could imply a Vanitas meaning; the decay of nature acting as a reminder of human frailty. However, the explanation could be natural, that the flowers wilted as the artist painted them and that the leaves had been eaten away, and the artist expresses realism rather than allegory. It is not possible to say whether this picture was executed in England or not as the artist's style did not change.

Caspar Netscher

Heidelberg date unknown – The Hague 1684

Netscher's reputation has always rested on *The Lace Maker* in the Wallace Collection, but the simplicity and directness of that picture is uncharacteristic of Netscher's work. He was principally a portraitist who executed a number of elaborate genre pieces as well. These genre pictures are typical of the 1660s and 1670s when greater attention to detail was sometimes achieved at the expense of composition and tonal unity. With the exception of *The Lace Maker*, Netscher's genre pictures are hardly innovative as they are derived from Terborch, Frans van Mieris and Godfried Schalcken. Netscher's portraiture has been little studied and many of the sitters he depicted have remained unidentified. These numerous portraits are usually painted competently but the characterisation can be weak. Netscher rarely achieved that mysterious dignity which Terborch gave to his sitters.

36. Portrait of a Lady, 1658
panel; 23.5 × 18.4 cm
National Loan Collection Trust, Cannon Hall Museum, Barnsley Metropolitan Borough Council

36

This picture, dated as early as 1658, shows that Netscher's portrait style, which he continued for the rest of the century, had already been evolved. The feeling of well-dressed comfort without ostentation is characteristic and one that the artist only abandoned in special circumstances, such as commissions for portraits of foreign royalty. Although he visited both France and Italy, most of Netscher's career was spent in The Hague where patronage increased after the consolidation of the Stadholder's power following the French invasion of the United Provinces in 1672.

Godfried Schalcken
Made near Geertruidenberg 1643 – The Hague 1706

Schalcken gained the patronage of the Stadholder Willem III of Orange and retained it when he became William III of England, joint monarch with his Stuart wife Mary. Schalcken's success has not been matched by his subsequent reputation. In fact Schalcken was one of the most skilled and inventive artists of his

37 [colour plate XXIX]

38

39

generation painting in a style rather different from that of his even more successful contemporary Adriaen van der Werff. Schalcken began his career with small elaborately detailed genre pieces in the style of Caspar Netscher, but soon found his true *métier* – the candlelight piece. He worked equally easily on the miniature scale preferred by many patrons as on the larger scale. He was also a distinguished portraitist painting in what can be loosely termed the international style of the time, which was a mixture of French and Netherlandish elements.

37. Self-Portrait by Candlelight
canvas; 109.8 × 88.8 cm
Warwick District Council Museum Service, Leamington Spa Art Gallery
Dutch 17th-century artists often painted themselves in individual self-portraits or as 'characters' in other pictures (Rembrandt and Jan Steen are examples of this). Dutch self-portraits are, however, rare in British collections and, apart from the Rembrandts in London, Liverpool and Glasgow, this is one of the few. Schalcken has shown himself by candlelight, even more dramatically than usual. He is in the fashionable 'undress' of the time with open shirt. More unusual is the gesture, towards the palette, and the wistful expression.

Gerard Hoet
Zalt Bommel 1648 – The Hague 1738

In terms of style and subject-matter, Hoet is comparable with Gérard de Lairesse (p.152). They were both influenced by contemporary French classical art although Hoet concentrated more on landscape elements derived from Gaspard Dughet. He also painted some quite different low-life genre pieces which usually betray the influence of near-by Rotterdam artists such as Cornelis Saftleven.

Hoet's son, Gerard Hoet II, was responsible for a compilation of early sale catalogues which was published in the middle years of the 18th century and is an invaluable source when tracing the histories of Dutch pictures in the previous hundred years.

38. Landscape with Pan and Syrinx
canvas; 38.3 × 47.5 cm

39. Landscape with Apollo and Daphne
canvas; 38.4 × 47.3 cm
Reproduced by permission of the Governors of the Dulwich Picture Gallery
These pictures form a matching pair complementary in subject. (Pairs could be contrasted as, for example, in Jan Steen's *Lean* and *Fat Kitchens* at Cheltenham Art Gallery.) Both pictures reflect the same mood and subject – in this case from Ovid's *Metamorphoses* – a hapless female, pursued by a lustful god, saved from indignity and rape by transformation into a plant (Daphne into a laurel and Syrinx into a reed bed). The poetical treatment of the landscape complements the story. This is an innovation in Dutch painting derived from a study of French classical landscapists, especially Gaspard Dughet (who had himself derived his approach from Nicolas Poussin). Dutch painters generally introduced landscapes into the background of their subject pictures as a decorative adjunct and not as part of the meaning of the picture. These two small paintings represent the end of the great tradition of Dutch landscape painting. Innovations in the 18th century were largely confined to townscape and genre painting.

Zwolle–Deventer–Hoorn–Gorinchem

The remoter Provinces, especially Overijssel, Gelderland and Groningen, were far from the mainstream of Dutch painting although such a popular picturesque site as Nijmegen in Gelderland was painted by Aelbert Cuyp, Jan van Goyen and Anthony Jansz. van der Croos. None of the towns in these provinces was really big enough to support a flourishing school of painting but there were dramatic exceptions. The twin towns of Zwolle and Kampen had two major painters working in the locality both at the beginning and at the end of the century. Hendrick Avercamp, the talented but essentially conservative winter-scene painter, worked in Kampen for part of his career often using the town walls as backgrounds to his skating scenes. One of the greatest Dutch genre painters, Gerard Terborch, was born in Zwolle but spent much of his career elsewhere. Zwolle provided the subject of one of the late masterpieces of Dutch painting, Hendrick ten Oever's *View of Zwolle* (p.74) which is as unique in the context of the artist's work as of the period in general. There can be no rational explanation for such a brief expression of genius in the work of a painter who otherwise remained obstinately mediocre. Exactly the reverse is true of Terborch who retained the highest standards throughout his long career. His mastery of genre and portraiture is unusual in the local context. He appears to have had no pupils or imitators besides his short-lived children.

A number of other centres have been overlooked in this survey because they are sparsely represented in British collections. Most of the pictures painted in Gouda in south Holland, especially the portraits, have remained there and the same is largely true of Hoorn in north Holland. The token representation of a Hoorn artist (Withoos, p.74) reveals the expected eccentricity away from the mainstream, whereas the modest picture from Gorinchem (p.75) is indicative of the occasional lower standards found in the smaller places.

Gerard Terborch

Zwolle 1617 – Deventer 1681

Of all the painters who spent part of their career away from a main centre, Terborch is the most refined and sophisticated. He spent part of his career in Zwolle and Deventer where there were few other active painters of talent. His genre paintings are among the finest of the period, both for their technical ability with silks and satins and for their uncanny ability to catch typical expressions. So many painters of the period created what is in essence a theatrical tableau in which every figure is an actor in a dream. Terborch realised that some people are unwilling actors and therefore some of his figures appear indifferent to the scene they are in. This makes for a much greater realism. His portraits combine austerity of colour and composition with great psychological penetration. They are almost always on a small scale.

40. A Dancing Couple
canvas; 76.2 × 67.2 cm
The National Trust, Polesden Lacey (Greville Collection)
This is one of the finest of Terborch's pictures and represents the height of refinement in Dutch genre painting. The gesture and pose of the dancing couple in this picture are perfectly observed. The artist has concentrated on the effect of the sheen on the silk dress which even overshadows the achievement of Gabriel Metsu (p.61). Indeed compared to the Metsu, where there is a strong psychological interest, the Terborch seems almost empty with the emphasis on gesture rather than specific mood. In his last years the artist resisted the harder style preferred in Leiden by Frans van Mieris and his pupils.

41. Portrait of Hendrick Casimir II, Prince of Nassau-Dietz, 1670
canvas; 33.4 × 27.8 cm
Manchester City Art Galleries
The artist shows the twelve-year-old prince in all his finery. Even so the rich colours, particularly the reds, are characteristically understated. As a portraitist Terborch excelled because his grasp of human character, so obvious in the genre pieces, came to the fore in his portraits. This boy has a determined mouth and sly-looking eyes with an aristocratic bearing (the Nassau-Dietz family were related to the Princes of Orange). Dutch portraits of the time, especially those of Terborch, express so subtly the essence of character without resorting to the passion of a Rembrandt or the bravura of Hals.

Hendrick ten Oever

Zwolle 1639 – Zwolle 1716

The art of Hendrick ten Oever gives weight to the hypothesis that in the smaller centres artists had to be less specialised and that without competition from other specialists they turned their hands to whatever subject their clients required. Ten Oever painted portraits and genre as well as landscapes and animal pieces. Most of these pictures reveal a modest and, in the wrong sense of the word, provincial quality. (It must be remembered that a number of the provincial centres

40

such as Dordrecht and Middelburg produced artists whose standards were equal to those in the larger cities.) Ten Oever's current reputation is based on one picture (see below), although a number of his animal pieces in the setting sun with long shadows also betray some originality.

41 [colour plate XXX]

42 [colour plate XXVI]

43 [colour plate XXVIII]

42. Evening Landscape with a distant View of Zwolle, 1675
canvas; 66.7 × 87 cm
University of Edinburgh (Torrie Collection)
This picture is justly celebrated as a unique vision of an evening landscape. Not until the early 19th century with Caspar David Friedrich was this crystalline, almost surreal, approach rivalled. The eerie effect is enhanced by the distant skyline of the town of Zwolle (before one of the main church towers collapsed). The subject of men bathing occurs again from time to time in Dutch painting of the period (Nicolaes Maes and Sweerts being good examples). No particular significance should be attached to this subject; it is but one of the myriad ways in which the Dutch recorded aspects of their everyday lives.

Matthias Withoos

Amersfoort 1627 – Hoorn 1703

In spite of his obvious ability, Withoos remains an obscure figure. He specialised in the 'forest floor' type of landscape pictures but his pictures are less populated by animals, insects and reptiles than those of Otto Marseus van Schrieck who originated the genre (p.148). Withoos was particularly responsive to the decorative effects of noxious plants – thistles, burdocks and deadly nightshade. Often one suspects that there is an underlying Vanitas theme – the triumph of nature over man. He also painted a few port scenes in a rather more conventional Italianate manner.

44

43. Thistles and Butterflies
canvas; 87.6 × 69.2 cm
Nottingham Castle Museum and Art Gallery
This complex picture needs to be interpreted on several different levels. On the first level it is a masterpiece of decorative effect with the patterns of dock leaves and thistles dominating. On a second, didactic level, the butterfly perhaps symbolises the shortness of human existence. All the plants are inimical to the cultivation of food or beautiful flowers, while the butterflies have developed from caterpillars which have already partly consumed the leaves in the foreground.

Johannes Meerhout

?Gorinchem date unknown – Amsterdam 1677

The career of Meerhout is largely undocumented but his pictures suggest that he spent some of his career in Gorinchem (Gorkum) where he was born. Gorinchem is not far from Dordrecht and not, therefore, geographically close to the other centres grouped together here, but was artistically 'remote'. Meerhout's style was derived from the early work of Jan van Goyen, *ie* rapid execution with the brush, and a tendency towards monochrome. As he was not an innovator and as his pictures are modest in scale, his art is ignored in general surveys of the period.

44. View of Gorinchem
panel; 30.4 × 37.4 cm
Leicestershire Museum and Art Gallery, Leicester
This small landscape is more than topography as the artist has used the town as a vehicle to express a particular mood. There is no loving description of the Gothic details of the churches but instead a concentration on an overall greyness of tone which conjures up the atmosphere of a grey but calm day.

Friesland

The Province of Friesland was the most remote from the rich and populous State of Holland. Sea connections were good and Friesland had a number of flourishing small ports such as Harlingen and Sneek. As the Province was largely surrounded by water, economic life, as in Zeeland, was concentrated on seafaring. Artistic activity in the smaller towns was limited and only the capital, Leeuwarden, supported a group of painters.

Most Frisian painters were portraitists and their works have usually remained in local collections. In their bold primitiveness many of these works resemble their Elizabethan and Jacobean counterparts, indeed many remain unrecognised, especially if they have no easily identifiable inscriptions or coats of arms.

The very remoteness of Leeuwarden preserved it from a weak imitation of the styles in fashionable large centres and caused painters to evolve strongly independent styles which were only appreciated locally. The Fries Museum of Leeuwarden has the only collection in existence which covers the whole period, and from this it is possible to see that almost all the genres were represented if not throughout the whole century.

Local idiosyncrasy reached its height in the painter Margarethe de Heer who is represented at Leeuwarden by meticulous studies of insects and the genre piece here (p.77) comes as a great surprise.

45

Adriaen van der Linde
Bruges date unknown – Bolsward 1609

The researches of Dr A Wassenberghe have brought to light a group of portraitists working in the remote Province of Friesland in the 16th and 17th centuries; van der Linde, who settled in Leeuwarden, the capital, originated in Flanders. He also worked in near-by Bolsward where he died. His pupils and followers included Jan de Salle and Pieter Feddes Harlingensis. Van der Linde and his pupils employed a hieratic style comparable to Elizabethan portraiture in Britain. Outside Friesland the whole school of painting remains little known and pictures from it are often given to artists from elsewhere.

Attributed to Adriaen van der Linde
45. A Boy with a Rattle
canvas; 68.8 × 53.2 cm
Leicestershire Museum and Art Gallery, Leicester
Although this picture was given to Leicester by Sir William Burrell (who included only a few but outstanding Dutch pictures in his gift to Glasgow) it has remained unidentified. The style is clearly Frisian and comes closest to Adriaen van der Linde. The attribution is based on a similarity with van der Linde's few signed portraits and his characteristic treatment of the hands with the dimples by the knuckles. It was the custom to dress children rather formally, boys as well as girls in long skirts. In Frisian painting they frequently carry elaborate toy rattles ('rinkelbel') which had decorative potential for the artist.

Petrus Schotanus
Dronrijp 1610 – Dronrijp or Leeuwarden 1662/75

In common with many of the artists who worked in Friesland, the career of Schotanus is undocumented and his pictures are rare. Apart from still-life painting on which his reputation rests, he also produced a few landscapes and portraits. The still-life pictures are almost always Vanitas pieces painted in monochrome. They are boldy executed and stand apart from the normal paintings by artists in the remoter provinces, who generally worked with painstaking detail.

46

46. Vanitas
panel; 59.7 × 82.5 cm
Maidstone Museum (Bentlif Collection)
Many Dutch still-lifes include a Vanitas element whether a discreetly-placed watch or hour-glass or contained in the symbolic meaning of certain flowers. This is an example of the rarer straight Vanitas referring to a range of human activities – learning (the book), hunting (the dead birds), military matters (standard) – piled up pell-mell on a ledge set rather improbably against a landscape. Among other symbols are the hour-glass, the globe with the signs of the zodiac and, hardly noticed on the left, the extinguished candle. The Vanitas was a timely reminder of mortality for one of the most materialistic societies the world had yet seen. Prosperity reached the remoter regions too, even though Friesland never enjoyed the mercantile wealth of cities in the Province of Holland.

Margarethe de Heer

working Friesland *c.*1620-*c.*1661

In common with a good number of women artists of the period, biographical details of Margarethe de Heer are scant. Her work is little known even though her few surviving pictures exhibit a high degree of skill. She seems to have been a specialist in the painting of insects – a more Flemish than Dutch accomplishment (*eg* Jan van Kessel). She worked in gouache on paper which produces a very light tonal effect. As her paintings were usually mounted on panel, they were intended to be displayed as pictures and not kept in an album like finished drawings.

47. Two Beggars fighting
paper on panel; 36.2 × 28.6 cm
Leicestershire Museum and Art Gallery, Leicester
Recent cleaning has revealed the high quality of this detailed

47

48

work. The subject was uncommon in Friesland where there appears to have been very little demand for genre painting of any type. A priest raising his hands in shock at the violence of the fighting beggars, narrowly escapes a basket flying through the air. Priests, rare in Dutch 17th-century painting, appear as a satirical element. The whole picture betrays great originality of approach even down to the delicate treatment of the large tree in the centre.

Wigerus Vitringa

Leeuwarden 1657 – Leeuwarden 1725

Vitringa is little known today as he worked in the remote Province of Friesland and only a handful of his works have been identified. He followed in the tradition of the van de Veldes and Bakhuizen. He also painted a few Italianate scenes and one exotic picture of the Arctic (see above).

48. A Bear Hunt in the Arctic, 1696
canvas; 44.5 × 57 cm
National Maritime Museum
Although the Dutch had built up a commercial world empire by the mid-17th century, representations of it are remarkably rare (*eg* p.95 for a Brazilian subject). The Dutch exploited the Arctic regions for fish and game and hence this unusual depiction of a bear hunt among the ice floes. As might be expected for a painter working away from the main centres, the technique is less refined and detailed but such boldness of conception and freshness of approach to the subject is often found in the work of Friesland painters.

Haarlem

Haarlem differed in some respects from other main Dutch cities. Physically it was dominated by the late-medieval church of St Bavo, known locally as the Grote Kerk or Great Church. The city was not the seat of a university like Leiden, Utrecht and Amsterdam (universities also existed in Groningen and at Franeker in Friesland). It had no direct access to the North Sea and ships had to travel through miles of inland waters to reach the city. Haarlem therefore did not develop into the great trading centre that its near neighbour Amsterdam became, nor did it have the ecclesiastical importance of Utrecht.

All these factors seem to have contributed to the remarkably insular development of the Haarlem school. The specific flavour of Haarlem school paintings is strong and can be caught more easily because of the high rate of survival of certain types of pictures. Unlike Rotterdam and Amsterdam, Haarlem was not prosperous in the 18th and 19th centuries and as a result the city retains its medieval and 17th-century atmosphere to this day. Group portraits of the guardians of almshouses and hospitals and of the officers of contemporary militia companies are still preserved in the city and they give us a uniquely concentrated view of this type of picture. Statistically, of course, the largest surviving number of group portraits comes from Amsterdam but it is in Haarlem that this specifically Dutch genre can best be studied and appreciated. Few of these pictures have left the locations for which they were painted and today a good number of them are gathered in the Frans Hals Museum, Haarlem, itself a former almshouse. Qualitatively the whole is dominated by Frans Hals whose eight group portraits span some fifty years of the artist's career. There are examples by many other artists ranging from a rather stilted work by Cornelis van Haarlem to the accomplished works of Verspronck whose reputation was greater than that of Hals at the time.

Unlike many other centres where there was a dominant or pervasive character – Dou in Leiden or Cuyp in Dordrecht – the Haarlem school of painting is remarkable for its variety as well as for its sobriety of colour and subject-matter which gives Haarlem pictures their specific flavour. Still-life, for instance, was almost always austere with very little colour added, a few sumptuous banquet pieces apart, and most of them concentrate on a few silver vessels or half-eaten pies. Even though such pictures typify one aspect of Dutch still-life painting (the chief exponents being Pieter Claesz., Willem Claesz., Heda and Gerrit Willemsz. Heda), they are rare in British collections.

Portraiture was the dominant subject in Haarlem but it was in the field of landscape painting that Haarlem artists were to achieve a national, even international, significance. They responded directly to the local landscape, especially to the nearby sand dunes, and only occasionally made concessions to the much more fashionable Italianate manner which was dominant in Utrecht. Some Haarlem artists such as Berchem (p.90) painted both realistic and Italianate landscapes, sometimes combining the two. Generally, however, Haarlem created a tradition of landscape painting that developed along a definable line. This too is in contrast to Utrecht where each generation took on a new wave of foreign influence. The early landscapes of Esaias van de Velde (p.88) and Pieter de Molijn gave way to the more naturalistic approach of Salomon van Ruysdael (p.91) and the high peak of achievement was reached with Jacob van Ruisdael (p.92). There were also many cross currents, for example in highly original works by Philips Wouwermans who painted dunes, battle pieces and hunting scenes. His pictures had an elegance and lightness of tone and colour which appealed to 18th-century taste.

The only area where there can be said to be strong outside influence was in genre painting. The catalyst was the Antwerp genre painter Adriaen Brouwer who spent some time in Haarlem in the 1630s. He imported a manner of painting peasant genre with broad free brushstrokes in brown tones contained within a small scale. His manner was adopted by several Haarlem genre painters, especially Adriaen van Ostade (p.87) who was the most important of them. Almost all Haarlem genre is derived from this one type of picture; elegant interiors, familiar from Leiden and Amsterdam, were strangers to Haarlem.

Subject painting held an honourable position at the end of the 16th century when Cornelis van Haarlem was commissioned to paint some important mythological pictures for the town hall. In the 17th century, subject painting declined although painters such as Cesar van Everdingen (p.81) and Pieter de Grebber continued to paint mythological and religious pieces.

Topography was especially popular in Haarlem. Berckheyde painted most of his pictures in and around the city (p.102) and Jacob van Ruisdael (p.93) based some of his most beautiful works on distant views of St Bavo. The greatest of all architectural painters, Pieter

49

Jansz. Saenredam, also worked for much of his career in Haarlem and about half his output concerns Haarlem churches and St Bavo in particular. Saenredam's obsessive interest in perspective and the fall of light meant that his pictures rise above topography in the accepted sense of the term.

The preference in Haarlem for some subjects rather than others means that a balanced history of Dutch painting by subject-matter could not be written round Haarlem painters, although after Amsterdam the city supported the largest colony of artists throughout the century. (It should also be emphasised that in the case of Amsterdam a good number of the painters were not local in origin and tended to arrive from other centres, their styles already mature.)

Cornelis Verbeeck

Haarlem 1590 – Haarlem ? 1633

Verbeeck's output consists mostly of rather small and clumsy shore scenes and seascapes. His ships rarely achieve the accuracy or delicacy of such important Haarlem contemporaries as the Vrooms, father and son. The picture included here is an exceptional work for Verbeeck suggesting that more pictures in the penumbra of the Vroom family may well turn out to be by him.

49. The Departure of Admiral Houtman's Fleet for the East Indies, 1623
canvas; 82 × 153 cm
Cheltenham Art Gallery
This picture records a specific event which took place in 1593/94 when Admiral Houtman departed for the East Indies in four small ships. The ships here are no doubt unhistorically grand, hardly surprising given that the picture was painted almost thirty years after the event. It is Verbeeck's most ambitious picture and lacks his usual naïveté in the treatment of the water. The general composition with its strong horizontal sweep is much indebted to Hendrick Cornelis Vroom.

Cesar Boetius van Everdingen

Alkmaar 1617 – Alkmaar 1678

Cesar van Everdingen was the chief representative of a style known as Haarlem Classicism. This hybrid kind of classical inspiration in the 1630s was shared by the Utrecht Caravaggesques, especially Jan Bijlert (p.48). Most of van Everdingen's pictures are bland treatments of classical or religious subjects painted with a light palette and in a style which he must have evolved in

50

Utrecht where he is recorded in 1632 as a Guild member. Most of his career was spent in Haarlem although his most important commission (from Amalia von Solms) was to decorate a residence of the House of Orange – the Huis ten Bosch at The Hague. This ambitious work shows Everdingen in command of an international style not to be anticipated from his work on a more modest scale. A considerable proportion of the artist's surviving output is portraiture, a series of portraits in the Stedelijk Museum at Alkmaar being outstanding.

50. Allegory of Winter
canvas; 91.8 × 71.2 cm
Southampton City Art Gallery
This is a mysterious and enigmatic picture which seems to anticipate Vermeer of Delft in its quiet reflection and perfect technique. The figure warming her hands over a bowl of hot charcoal is usually interpreted as an allegory of winter. The refinement of the proportions of the face represents a classicising tendency away from Dutch realism. This occurs in Vermeer's work too, especially in two single heads of young women (The Hague, Mauritshuis, and New York, Metropolitan Museum). Such a haunting image is rarely found among the Haarlem Classicists who were generally more robust and homespun in their approach.

51. A Boy with a Sheep, 1639
canvas; 99 × 78.7 cm
The National Trust, Polesden Lacey (Greville Collection)
The inclusion of the sheep is a not uncommon feature of mid-century portraits when there was an interest in the pastoral ideal inspired by poetry. This type of subject was especially fashionable in Utrecht. Van Everdingen's bold style is unmistakable, especially in the treatment of the face, although the picture was for long attributed to Aelbert Cuyp. The portrait at Barnsley (see below) painted twenty-five years later shows a marked stylistic and technical advance.

52. A Child holding an Apple, 1664
canvas; 100.2 × 83.9 cm
National Loan Collection Trust, Cannon Hall Museum, Barnsley Metropolitan Borough Council
It has been suggested that this child is Maria Baert, daughter of the Burgomaster of Alkmaar, who was baptised there in December 1661 and this would fit the date on the picture. Van Everdingen's normal portrait style is more austere and this picture adopts the light tones of his subject pictures. It is likely that the considerable property in the background (again an unusual feature for Everdingen) represents the child's family home with its neatly tended avenue of trees. There may be some significance in the fact that the child is holding a finch. Curiously, child portraiture becomes increasingly rare in Dutch painting after the middle years of the century.

Dirck Hals
Haarlem 1591 – Haarlem 1656

Dirck Hals was the younger brother of Frans Hals and the latter's greatness has contributed to an underestimation of the former's achievement as the innovator of a particular genre. The earliest artist to paint low-life interior scenes was the Rotterdam artist Willem Buytewech from whose hand only a few pictures survive. Dirck Hals developed this subject into a fully-fledged genre with its own conventions. His compositions are almost always in a long and narrow horizontal format. Paintings hang in the background and the company is generally engaged in discreet merriment. This type of genre was taken up by several painters of a slightly younger generation, including Pieter Codde (p.129) and Palamedes (p.106).

53. Dutch Party of Cavaliers and Ladies
panel; 43.2 × 78.4 cm
Nottingham Castle Museum and Art Gallery

51

52

53

This is an excellent example of an early 'middle-class' genre piece which was to dominate from mid-century until it went out of fashion around 1660. The social historian may take such subjects for the 17th-century equivalent of a cocktail party. It seems to have been perfectly acceptable in company for even people of quality to fondle one another amorously. Also characteristic was the habit of leaning back on chairs (a habit forbidden to generations of children to this day). In the background is a seascape in an austere black frame, often used at this period, although after the middle years of the century gilt was increasingly employed for picture frames. The map depicts the Dutch Republic as usual turned on its side with North on the right. Such maps appear, very much more carefully painted, in the work of Vermeer of Delft.

Frans Hals

Antwerp ?*c.*1580 – Haarlem 1666

Hals is placed second in the trio of great Dutch 17th-century painters with Rembrandt first and Vermeer third. This ranking is a very recent one in the history of taste; Vermeer was not rediscovered until the 1860s and Hals not recognised as one of the great Dutch painters until the late-19th century. Hals' art is much more complex and various than is popularly understood from his single and group portraits because his genre pieces and two religious works form a very small proportion of his total *œuvre*. In fact a career of some fifty years saw considerable stylistic changes. His earliest group portraits (all at Haarlem) belong to the 16th-century tradition – one of them had its composition taken over from Cornelis van Haarlem. His single portraits were conventional too – note, for instance, *Man with a Skull* (Birmingham, Barber Institute) which takes over both composition and style from the Burgher Portrait of the Leiden school from Exeter (p.56). From these conventional beginnings around 1610 in Haarlem, Hals changed rapidly introducing the free brushwork for which he has been admired in modern times but which offended 18th-century connoisseurs. In 1624 the artist painted his now most famous picture *The Laughing Cavalier* (London, Wallace Collection). In the 1630s and 1640s Hals' art became more austere and his palette more restrained. This did not affect his freedom of brushwork, however, and in his last pictures painted around 1660 he seems to be at his freest. Perhaps his greatest works, especially for their psychological penetration, are the two last group portraits, *The Regents and Regentesses of the Old Women's Alms House in Haarlem* (Haarlem, Frans Hals Museum).

54 [colour plate IV]

54. A laughing Child holding a Flute (Sense of Hearing)

panel; diameter 29 cm

Private Collection, on loan to the Birmingham City Museum and Art Gallery

Hals must have executed a large number of small pictures of children with various expressions although modern scholarship, astonishingly, accepts as authentic only three of them. This one almost certainly formed part of a series of the five senses and although such series were very common in the 17th century very few of them have survived intact. Few examples of Hals' work show a greater liveliness and freedom of brushwork than this picture, which is very close in handling to a similar work in the Mauritshuis, The Hague. These pictures have been placed in the 1620s which is remarkably early for such freedom of handling. This painting is first recorded in the collection of Sir Alfred Beit, London, around 1900 (Hofstede de Groot, no.3; Slive, no.27).

55. Portrait of a smiling Woman

canvas; 57.2 × 53.4 cm

Ferens Art Gallery : Hull City Museums and Art Galleries

This, one of Hals' most endearing female portraits, has only become well-known in recent years. Hals' style ranged from an incisive observation of human passion in the late group portraits to the rumbustuous moods of the Haarlem militia companies. Hals was rarely in contemplative mood as here, but clearly could capture subtlety as well as strength of character. The method of painting is, as usual with Hals, extremely direct without any complex build-up of layers as

55 [colour plate XVI]

56

57

59

58

is found in almost all Rembrandt's work. In such pictures, too, Hals used a very restrained palette avoiding local colour in the draperies. This picture has proved difficult to place in Hals' career but it is generally dated in the 1650s.

Jan de Bray
Haarlem 1626/27 ? – Haarlem 1697

The reputation of Jan de Bray has been overshadowed by his contemporaries in Haarlem who were able to paint with greater clarity. For group portrait painting it was undoubtedly Verspronck who had the greatest talent for the clear sober depiction of alert-looking burghers. De Bray used a less refined and bolder technique. He was, however, more important as a history painter continuing the tradition of Cesar van Everdingen and Pieter de Grebber at a time when their rather bland and classicising style had gone out of fashion in other centres. Jan de Bray remained uninfluenced by the stylistic changes which took place in the middle years of the century in Haarlem, especially by the achievement of Frans Hals in his late group portraits.

56. Portrait of a Dutch Gentleman aged 47, 1662
panel; 22.2 × 15.8 cm

57. Portrait of his Wife, aged 47, 1663
panel; 22.8 × 16.5 cm

58. Portrait of their elder Son, 1662
panel; 19.7 × 14 cm

59. Portrait of their younger Son, aged 7, 1663
panel; 19.7 × 14 cm
Trustees of the National Galleries of Scotland, Edinburgh
This group of family portraits is a rare survival from the period as even husband and wife pairs have so often been split up. The direct and realistic approach conforms to the 'Haarlem style' rather than being specifically influenced by Frans Hals, the most individual rather than the most typical of the Haarlem portrait painters. Typical of Haarlem taste is the absence of bold local colour. Such austerity is found in most bourgeois portraiture and group portraits with the signal exception of the militia groups in which strong colour abounds. Even though these pictures are on such a small scale, their realism is exactly that which inspired French painters of the mid-19th century from Courbet onwards.

60

60. Jael and Sisera, 1659
panel; 101.7 × 83.8 cm
York City Art Gallery
This picture contradicts most of the generalisations made in this book – namely that there is an identifiable local style. In fact artists such as Rembrandt had an influence as far away as Dordrecht through the medium of pupils. De Bray, a recognisably Haarlem artist, has produced a frankly Rembrandtesque picture. Rembrandt never painted the subject but there are several drawings by him of this violent Old Testament scene in which Jael kills Sisera by driving a tent peg through his temple. The artist has assimilated all the Rembrandtesque tricks of colour and brushwork and has even managed to bring off a sense of brooding violence which Rembrandt was able to achieve effortlessly.

Adriaen van Ostade
Haarlem 1610 – Haarlem 1685

Adriaen van Ostade was perhaps the most significant and certainly the most prolific of all Dutch 'low-life' genre painters. His style was formed in Haarlem under the influence of the Flemish painter Adriaen Brouwer whose brown tones and animated composition he imitated. Contrary to what might be expected from a painter who repeated the same theme many hundreds of times, the artist's work falls into several distinct categories. He sometimes used a rather highly-coloured

61

and meticulous style in contrast with a much freer and brownish-toned manner which is closer to Brouwer's. His descriptions of the human condition verge on caricature and lack the biting humour of Jan Steen. Nevertheless, at his best, his reputation as a genre painter is justified. One of the most important groups of his pictures is in the British Royal Collection.

61. Peasants drinking in an Interior
panel; 26.8 × 33 cm
Essex County Council, Chelmsford Shire Hall
Peasants tipple and canoodle with gusto in a tavern. Van Ostade treats his low-life subject with extreme refinement of composition and technique. Carefully thought-out is the balance of colour for the draperies and the treatment of gesture and expression. Even on a very small scale, Ostade's faces are readable as caricatures of the peasant type. The bright colour and bold brushwork indicate that the picture is likely to be an early work as later in his career the artist turned increasingly towards the inclusion of a large amount of minute detail.

Cornelis Pietersz. Bega

Haarlem 1631/32 – Haarlem 1664

Bega represents the tradition of refined genre painting in Haarlem rather than the coarser variety preferred by Adriaen van Ostade and his followers such as Cornelis Dusart. Bega's technique is easily recognisable; he liked to polish the painting surface in a way peculiar to himself and introduced unusual bluish-grey tones to the draperies. His extremely careful manner of painting limited his production and his pictures are relatively rare. His style changed little throughout his career.

62. Tavern Scene, 1662
canvas; 38.4 × 33.6 cm
York City Art Gallery
The exquisite technique which Bega applies to this low-life scene is usually reserved for middle-class genre, little of which was produced in Haarlem. This picture can be interpreted either as a simple domestic interior or as a brothel scene, the rather slatternly woman reading the paper being ambiguous. The drinker is far gone!

Esaias van de Velde

Haarlem ?1590 – The Hague 1630

Esaias van de Velde was one of the first Dutch painters to produce landscapes of local scenery. He is considered to be the founder of the great Dutch school of landscape painting which culminated in van Ruisdael, Cuyp and Hobbema. His significance has sometimes been over-estimated, especially in the context of the Flemish (Southern Netherlandish) tradition of landscape painting which was brought into the Dutch Republic by such significant painters as Savery (p.43) and Vinckeboons. Nevertheless, Esaias van de Velde did establish his own landscape style which had no Flemish overtones and this was an important influence on the early work of Jan van Goyen, who was a pupil of his in Haarlem. Later van de Velde settled in The Hague where his art was not particularly influential as there was no school of landscape painting there. He also painted a few battle pieces which owe rather more to the Flemish tradition. Although he died young, Esaias van de Velde painted a relatively large number of pictures.

63. River Scene, 1623
panel; 29.2 × 48.4 cm
Reproduced without the addition at the top – see below
The Royal Pavilion, Art Gallery and Museums, Brighton
A strip of panel some 6 cm wide has been added to the top of this composition radically altering a claustrophobic and narrow picture, with the central tree touching the top, to a more open and conventional composition. Exactly the same thing has happened to the Hondecoeter from Dundee (p.45). Once the picture is reduced to its original dimensions in the mind's eye, the originality of the artist is at once obvious. Velde never followed the convention of the brown, blue-green palette favoured by Savery and most of the other Flemish artists in the Dutch Republic. Instead he preferred a much more naturalistic palette of greys and grey-greens. This choice was favoured by the young van Goyen, who also took over Velde's brightly-coloured figures. The composition of the Brighton picture is bold and original, uniting the rustic

62

63

scene on the left with the river scene on the right. Great attention is paid to the horizon which was favoured by Jan van Goyen in his maturity.

Nicolaes Berchem

Haarlem 1620 – Amsterdam 1685

Berchem was the son of the still-life painter Pieter Claesz. and the early sources give a number of painters as his teachers, including Jan van Goyen, Pieter de Grebber and Jan Baptist Weenix. Berchem was one of the most prolific of all the Dutch Italianate landscape painters and also the most esteemed of the group (which includes Jan Both and Aelbert Cuyp) in the 18th century. Berchem's style was remarkably varied, ranging from pictures strongly influenced by his local surroundings in Haarlem with open skies and sand dunes to the fully-fledged Italianate views which make no concessions to the North either in light or composition. It was assumed until recent times that Berchem acquired this skill in Italy, as did Poelenburgh (p.49), Breenbergh (p.127) and Asselijn. Modern scholarship argues for an Italian trip made in mid-career in the 1650s when the artist had already acquired his facility for porcelain-blue skies and horizons suffused with a golden glow. Berchem's Italianate landscapes filled with lively figures and animals were extremely influential and he was followed by a host of minor painters

64

such as Willem Romeyn and Aelbert Klomp and his 'manner' was employed by mediocre painters right through the 18th century.

64. Landscape with Herdsmen and Cattle
panel; 42 × 52 cm
Trustees of the Holburne Museum, Bath
Recent cleaning has revealed a good example of Berchem's more naturalistic manner. There is some artificiality in the composition but the colours are entirely Northern in their tone. Berchem was especially good at figures and animals and always painted his own in his pictures.

65

Anthony Jansz. van der Croos
? 1606/07 – The Hague 1662/63

Anthony Jansz. van der Croos came from a family of painters and his son, Jacob van der Croos, followed his style of painting. Both painters derived their ideas from Jan van Goyen's landscapes of the 1630s in which greens and browns predominate. There has been considerable confusion between the work of father and son because of the similarity of their signatures as well as of their painting style. The father's work tends to be more refined and his pictures often have a bluish tone which makes them appear slightly artificial in mood. Almost all the surviving pictures of both painters are of the Dutch countryside, particularly from around The Hague and Haarlem where they worked.

65. Landscape with the ruined Castle of Brederode and a distant View of Haarlem, 1655
panel; 48.2 × 66.5 cm
Shipley Art Gallery, Gateshead (Tyne and Wear Museums Service)

Innumerable topographical paintings survive of picturesque or ancient sites in the Dutch Republic, although for some reason such pictures were not particularly popular with British collectors. Many of van der Croos' pictures record, with a certain amount of artistic licence, castles and churches in The Hague/Haarlem area. The castle of Brederode, just outside Haarlem, was a favourite picturesque spot as it was within walking distance of the town; it was the subject of one of Hobbema's most elaborate and successful landscapes (London, National Gallery). As often with Croos, a delicate and airy technique invests the topographical scene with a particular mood.

Salomon van Ruysdael
Naarden 1602/03 – Haarlem 1670

After almost two centuries of neglect, the art of Salomon van Ruysdael has suddenly become more fashionable (to judge by the saleroom) than that of the far greater Jacob van Ruisdael. Salomon van Ruysdael was very close to van Goyen in his early years following his strong greenish-brown tonalities in river scenes. In the 1630s, however, the two artists diverged and Salomon van Ruysdael evolved the type of river-scene painting he was to practise for the next thirty years. The basic formula was naturalistic, often with scudding clouds seen against a clear cool blue. Then came the calm water, often with ferry boats and fishermen. The vegetation was constructed from conventions inspired by van Goyen's effortless calligraphy. Ruysdael did, however, make some original contribution to the developing genre of landscape painting. In addition he painted a few competent still-lifes.

66

66. River Scene with a distant View of Vianen, 1645
canvas; 77.5 × 114.3 cm
Leicestershire Museum and Art Gallery, Leicester
This picture has all Salomon van Ruysdael's clichés and formulae and is one of his most successful works of this type. He has attempted to give the picture a sense of place – in this case Vianen on the River Lek, one of the distributaries of the Rhine. The artist has also achieved the feeling of openness and breadth which characterises the Dutch landscape. If we follow the river bank to the right, we reach the spot from which Aelbert Cuyp made another view of Vianen at about the same time (p.124).

Jacob van Ruisdael
Haarlem 1628 – Amsterdam 1682

Jacob van Ruisdael has always been highly esteemed by connoisseurs of art and poetical appreciation by Goethe has given the artist a literary position rare for Dutch 17th-century painters. However, despite a recent exhibition in the Netherlands and the USA which brought together a selection of his best works, and in spite of the fact that the best single collection of his work is in the National Gallery, London, his reputation is *lower* today than at any point in the last three hun-

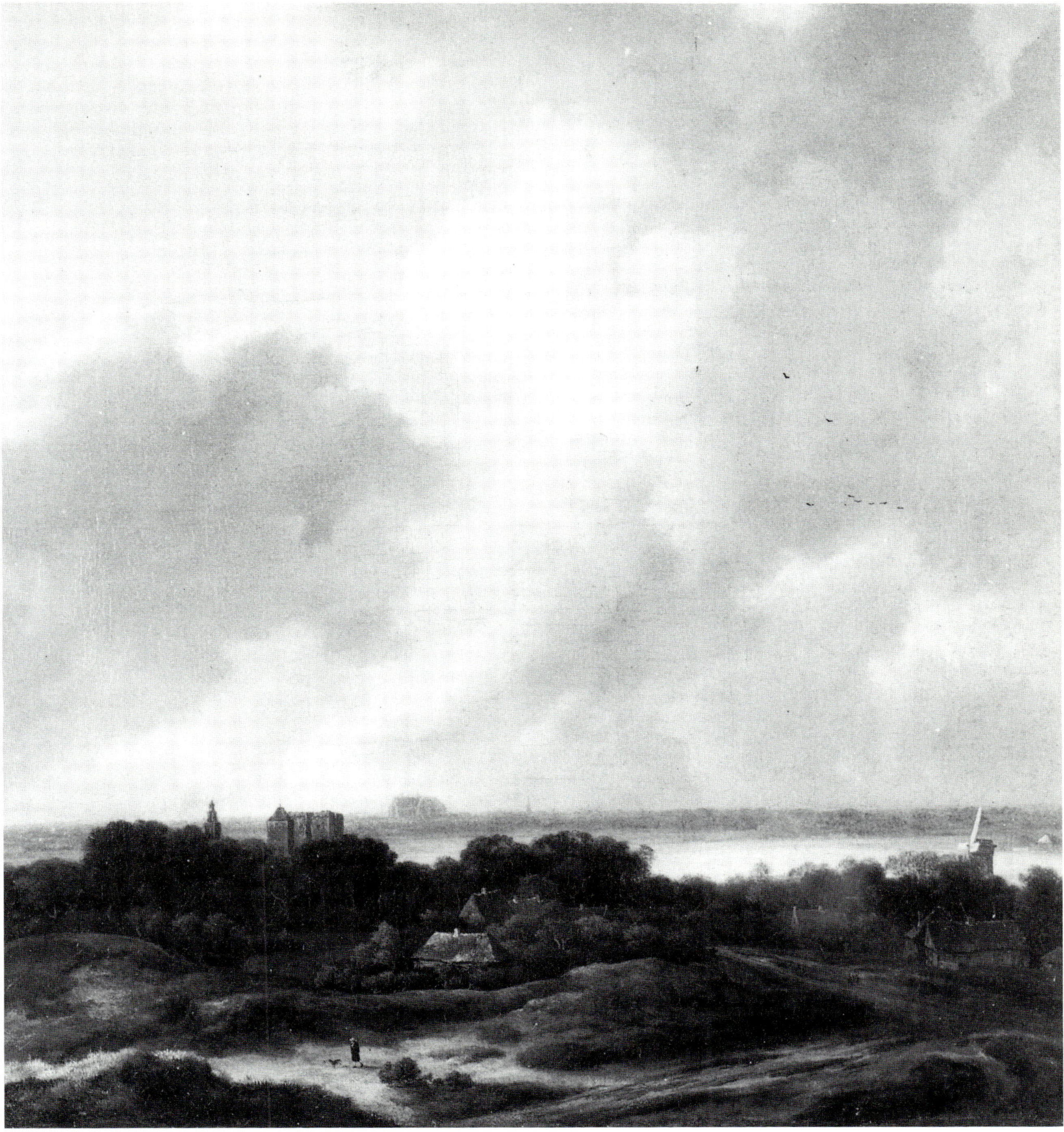

67

dred years. Of all Dutch landscape painters he is the only one who was able to give landscape an emotional and moral content, elevating him to the rank of a great artist. This was perceived early on but modern taste does not respond to Ruisdael's exquisite melancholy or to his use of grey and black shadows which betray a preoccupation with the futility of man's life before the inexorable forces of nature. Such depth of poetry is considered jejune by late 20th-century intellectuals and gloomy by the late 20th-century entrepreneurial classes who buy art. Ruisdael's sensitivity to landscape and his powers of composition raise him far above any other Dutch landscape painter of the time. He was influential both upon his contemporaries (Jan Looten, Jan van Kessel, Cornelis Decker, Meindert Hobbema, p.142) and upon 18th-century British artists, including Gainsborough.

Ruisdael was remarkably various in his approach. He painted woodland scenes primarily but also waterfalls in mountainous landscapes, cornfields, views of Haarlem with magnificent skies, and a small group of perfectly considered townscapes of Amsterdam. It is not extravagant to claim him as one of the greatest of all landscape artists.

67. Landscape with a distant View of Haarlem (*Le Coup de Soleil*)
canvas; 40 × 48 cm
The National Trust, Upton House (Bearsted Collection)
Although this is certainly a distant view of Haarlem, the picture has been dated to the 1670s when the artist was living in nearby Amsterdam. The view is the same as that depicted by van der Croos (p.91) although its treatment could not be more different. The silhouette of the building on the left is meant to be the ruined castle of Brederode but the interest is focused on the splendour of the sky with its piled-up clouds and shaft of sunlight. The topography has been used as an excuse for a panoramic landscape on a small scale where the space seems enhanced rather than diminished by the fact that the canvas is only just over one foot wide.

68. A River in Spate
canvas; 66.9 × 54.2 cm
Bristol City Art Gallery
Although this is an austere work, it lacks the profound melancholy of a number of Ruisdael's waterfall scenes. It is not known whether Ruisdael visited such a mountainous region or whether he relied on his imagination. The endlessly falling water can be seen as an expression of the timelessness of

68

nature and the moral frailty of man. Ruisdael's landscapes are often imbued with such moral ideals, the purest expression of which is found in the two versions (Dresden and Detroit) of *The Jewish Cemetery*. The Bristol picture, although lacking the blackish tonality of the artist's most sombre works, betrays great sensitivity to nature.

Frans Post

Leiden 1612 – Haarlem 1680

Frans Post spent seven years (1637-44) in Brazil painting local scenes. The rest of his long career was spent in Haarlem where he continued to paint Brazilian scenes. His style of painting was inconsistent and ranged from a rather conventional Haarlem manner inspired by the Ruisdael family, but in Brazilian fancy dress, to something much more direct and personal. Some of these Brazilian scenes are starkly simple and self-consciously naïve – a character not attempted again in landscape until Douanier Rousseau. He was highly esteemed in his lifetime and for a short period after his death and a group of his works were acquired by Louis XIV of France. Post's reputation has revived in recent years after two centuries of neglect.

69. Iguaraçú, Church and Cloister
canvas; 43 × 58.5 cm
Private Collection
This is one of Frans Post's most minutely detailed and highly-coloured pictures, almost certainly painted after his return from Brazil in 1644 but accurately recording the appearance of a Portuguese settlement there. The composition is almost classical in its careful balance of the main elements and, apart from the exotic details, fits into the general pattern of Haarlem landscape painting at its height in the middle years of the century. Unusually for a landscape painter, Post was able to paint figures and animals convincingly and this even extended to such creatures as the armadillo seen in the lower right corner of the picture.

69

70

71

Thomas Wijk

Beverwijk 1616 – Haarlem 1677

Thomas Wijk began his career as an Italianate landscape painter more in the robust manner of Pieter van Laer than in the elegant landscape manner of Jan Both. He also painted marine and genre pieces. His most often repeated subject was the alchemist in his laboratory derived from the Flemish David Teniers the Younger. He spent some time in London after 1660 and was responsible for a series of compositions depicting the Great Fire of London in 1666.

70. Washerwomen at the Foot of a Tower
panel; 58.8 × 51.4cm
Ferens Art Gallery : Hull City Museums and Art Galleries
This picture is a typical example of unidealised Dutch Italianate townscape. There is very little concession given to compositional conventions. The tower, which dominates the composition with its mass, can be identified with the Torre delle Milizie, a building of Roman origin near Rome, which can also be seen in the distance in the painting by Breenbergh (p.128). The washerwomen in the foreground provide the anecdotal detail to this bold and daring composition.

Claes Molenaer

Haarlem 1620/30 – Haarlem 1676

Claes Molenaer's best works are his early ones which assimilate the austere landscape style of Jacob van Ruisdael, in particular that of his winter scenes. Remaining in Haarlem after the departure of Ruisdael for Amsterdam, Molenaer changed imperceptibly but inexorably into a painter of winter scenes which charm

72

but do not move. He had a knack of introducing the trivial, and by making the snow fall picturesquely, he managed to banish all Ruisdael's sense of the timeless. Even though he came close to banalities, Molenaer must be seen as a *typical* artist of the period – his work would have been easily marketable as he was prolific.

71. Winter Scene
canvas; 49.5 × 66 cm
Beecroft Art Gallery, Westcliff-on-Sea
Winter scenes of this type by several artists, including Aert van der Neer, must have been extremely popular to judge by the large numbers of them which survive. The elements are conventional enough, but they are painted with respect for nature. No particular town is described and Molenaer generalised all his skies repeating the same elements from picture to picture.

Jan Wijnants
Haarlem 1625 – Amsterdam 1684

Wijnants, though less various than Nicolaes Berchem, was a leading figure in landscape painting in Haarlem. His development was the reverse of Berchem's beginning with realistic dune scenes and ending with rather heavy Italian landscapes influenced by Jan Both as well as Berchem. The cause of this *volte face* in the 1670s, late in his career, was the sudden fashion for Italianate subjects. This resulted in a revival of the Poelenburgh style in other centres besides Haarlem, including The Hague and Utrecht.

It has often been said that the quality of Wijnants' landscapes is in inverse proportion to their size. Certainly it is true that the small pictures have an almost crystalline clarity and by comparison the larger ones appear muddy. The type of landscape he painted has now almost disappeared from the Dutch countryside because of further reclamation and the dunes are no longer covered with silver birch trees.

72. River Scene with Figures
canvas; 26.6 × 35.5 cm
Bristol City Art Gallery
This is a good example of Wijnants' hybrid style. At first glance the dunes and trees are convincing enough as the environs of Haarlem, the sky is cool enough to be Northern and the figures certainly seem Dutch. But as the eye follows the meandering river, it meets a 'foreign' building that does not belong to the Dutch countryside (it is also out of scale). The distant hills are hardly Dutch and have been imported to balance the composition and to contribute a feeling of pastoral elegance.

73 [colour plate XX]

Roelof van Vries
Haarlem 1631/32 – Amsterdam after 1681

Van Vries was a minor painter in the sense that he followed the landscape style of Jacob van Ruisdael in Haarlem without making any specific contribution of his own. His pictures are easily recognisable as he added his own slightly idiosyncratic treatment of the leaves which owes more to Ruisdael's pupil Hobbema than the master himself. In spite of their modest simplicity, the landscapes of van Vries occasionally achieve a mastery of mood anticipating 18th-century landscape paintings in England. Indeed, it is likely that such artists as Gainsborough and Crome looked at works by van Vries in the mistaken belief that they were either by Jacob van Ruisdael or Hobbema.

73. Travellers by a Village
panel; 60 × 85 cm
Birmingham City Museums and Art Gallery
This is one of van Vries' most ambitious and successful pictures which indicates his debt to the Haarlem tradition of landscape painting. In general mood the inspiration is from Jacob van Ruisdael but the handling, especially in the trees, is closer to Hobbema. Van Vries never had Ruisdael's sense of melancholy and this picture is a good example of the truly picturesque landscape (a type which was perfected by Wijnants in Haarlem as well (see opposite)). The arrangement of trees, dunes and distant landscape is characteristic of early Gainsborough.

74

Barend Gael
Haarlem 1630? – Amsterdam ?after 1681

Gael is a minor artist who comes at the end of the great tradition of painting in Haarlem. He was the pupil of Philips Wouwermans whose style he imitated without achieving the latter's lightness and delicacy. He also, in the treatment of his pictures, followed the standard Haarlem tradition typified by Adriaen van Ostade.

75

76

74. The Ford
panel; 55.8 × 45.1 cm
Birmingham City Museums and Art Gallery
Recent cleaning has revealed the delicate silvery tones of this painting which is derived in almost all its elements from Philips Wouwermans. The artist's treatment of both landscape and figures is usually somewhat cruder than this and the picture has the further interest of the bathers in the background. The picture is likely to be an early work *c.*1660.

Dirck de Bray

working Haarlem 1651, *d.* after 1676

Dirck de Bray was the son of Salomon de Bray and the brother of the much better-known Jan de Bray. The dates of his painting career are not precisely fixed. He worked in a variety of styles as befitted the wide variety of subjects he treated. He painted portraits, hunting still-lifes and Vanitas pieces. In the local context it was his flower pieces which were important as there were few flower painters in Haarlem. Dirck de Bray produced a small number of exquisitely-crafted and highly individual pieces in this genre.

75. Vase of Flowers
panel; 63.5 × 44.3 cm
Trustees of the Ormonde Collection on loan to the Harris Museum and Art Gallery, Preston
Even though this is a very simple still-life by the standards of Walscapelle or Rachel Ruysch, the treatment is especially lush. The peony on the right is painted with a regard to light and texture more typical of the 19th century than the 17th. The peonies, aquilegia (columbine), morning glory, snowball flower and, on the table, periwinkle, all bloom at the same time in late May and early June. The whole has the rare feeling of having been painted from life rather than pieced together from painstaking studies.

76. Basket of Summer Flowers
panel; 63.5 × 44.3 cm
Trustees of the Ormonde Collection on loan to the Harris Museum and Art Gallery, Preston
Like the previous painting to which it apparently forms a

77

pendant, this has every appearance of being painted from life. The flowers are arranged in the basket with remarkable casualness for the period and the artist has been able to demonstrate his ability with perspective. Note, for instance, the unusual angle from which the Dutch iris is seen. The other flowers are roses, lilies and hollyhocks. This and its companion have not been published previously.

Gerrit Berckheyde
Haarlem 1638 – Haarlem 1698

Gerrit Berckheyde is the most important of all the Haarlem topographical artists. He favoured the great central square of the town which is dominated by the Grote Kerk with the picturesque Stadhuis opposite it. His style was naturalistic with clear lighting and attention to detail. His pictures are quite different in mood to those of the obsessive Jan van der Heyden, whose approach was even more minutely detailed. Berckheyde's lighting is usually clear and cool and in this respect he was less expert than van der Heyden.

77. View of the Castle of Heemstede
canvas; 63 × 49.7 cm
Private Collection
This picture is a masterpiece of cool clarity showing how Berckheyde could control perspective, light and tone. Characteristically the main part of the building is in shadow but without obscuring all the architectural details. The picture is also interesting as it shows a substantial late-medieval building adapted to modern comforts and style. Windows have been enlarged and there has been an extension at the rear. The main entrance conforms to the fashion of the 17th century rather than earlier and there has been a major

reorganisation of the forecourt so as to introduce a fashionable balustrade. A more precisely painted version of this composition (dated 1667) was recently bequeathed to the City of London Mansion House (Harold Samuel Collection).

Pieter Jansz. Saenredam

Assendelft 1597 – Haarlem 1665

Saenredam is usually considered to be the greatest of all the Dutch church interior painters although he was not the most realistic. Most of his long career was spent in Haarlem and his visits to other centres, such as Utrecht and 's-Hertogenbosch, were brief and were made for the purpose of executing elaborate perspective drawings of the medieval churches. These were worked up into paintings sometimes with an interval of as much as twenty years between the drawing and the finished painting.

Apart from a few early works which include a *View of Rome* most of Saenredam's pictures are views of the interiors and exteriors of Dutch medieval churches. By careful manipulation of perspective Saenredam gave his churches a simplicity, clarity and grandeur which is found in no other Dutch architectural painter's work. Even though Saenredam's pictures sometimes seem spacious to the point of emptiness, detail is never omitted but is subordinated to the tonal unity of the whole. Except by Isaac van Nickelen (p.103), Saenredam was not imitated. This is probably because his pictures were too idiosyncratic to conform to the popular demand for realistic church interiors of the type painted by van Vliet (p.109).

78. Imaginary Church Interior
canvas; 109 × 103 cm
Private Collection
This is the only work by Saenredam which represents an imaginary church interior and therefore its interpretation is of some importance for an understanding of the way in which the artist evolved his unique style. It is likely to be an early work on grounds of general style and the treatment of the figures. Unfortunately the last two digits of the date following the signature on the balustrade are difficult to interpret and Swillens at the time of the picture's discovery in 1960 read the date improbably as 1641 although 1627 could be equally convincing. In creating this large-scale work the artist has introduced a number of elements familiar from the Gothic churches of North Holland, especially St Pieterskerk, Leiden, for the pillars, and the wooden vaulting is typical of many churches in the area from Gouda to Alkmaar. The surprise of the picture, however, is the way in which these familiar elements are manipulated into a vast space with changes of level

78 [colour plate VII]

and an enormous ground-plan. The illusion is of a huge basilican church with apsidal chapels which never existed in the Netherlands. With the exception of Edinburgh's *Interior of St Bavo, Haarlem* no other work by Saenredam is so ambitious. The style used is curious to the point of uniqueness as many of the elements appear almost calligraphic in their treatment and in themselves unlike most of the drawings which were much more often concerned with tonal relationships.

Even though the approach is essentially linear, the effect of the picture is monumental enough. The columns are defined by patches of sunlight falling on them and the artist has introduced a number of distortions in the perspective which emphasise the still understated drama of the scene.

Isaac van Nickelen

working Haarlem *c.*1660 - 1703

Relatively little is known about van Nickelen's career except that it was spent in Haarlem and that it is likely, on stylistic grounds, that he was the pupil of Pieter Jansz. Saenredam. Van Nickelen derived his compositions and colours from Saenredam but developed his own individual mood. Saenredam's church interiors are cool and detached and have an almost surreal atmosphere quite unlike the interiors of the churches they depict. Van Nickelen, on the other hand, who, unlike Saenredam, concentrated almost exclusively on St

Bavo in Haarlem, gave these interiors a more comfortable feel by reducing the vast spaces of St Bavo into something more akin to a parish church. Van Nickelen's work is relatively rare like that of other church interior specialists with the possible exception of van Vliet (p. 109).

79. Interior of St Bavo, Haarlem
canvas; 47.5 × 40 cm
Birmingham City Museums and Art Gallery
The composition of this painting is closely related to Saenredam's *Interior of St Bavo, Haarlem* (Philadelphia Museum of Art, Johnson Collection). Saenredam executed the drawing (Haarlem, Gemeente Archief) for this painting in 1629 although the Johnson picture is probably very much later. Van Nickelen must have known either Saenredam's painting or the drawing or both as he follows these rather than what he could see by direct observation in the church. In van Nickelen's hand the uncompromising nature of Saenredam's vision is unsubtly modified by reducing the space to manageable proportions, by introducing the curiously-scaled pews which dwarf the figures. These factors imply that the picture is an early work by van Nickelen before he became more independent from Saenredam.

The church itself, a favourite subject for Haarlem painters, has altered little in its basic structure since Saenredam's drawing. A vast organ was introduced later in the 17th century in front of the great west window, completely changing the lighting effect in the nave. The nave, shown here looking east, is no longer filled with pews and in reality is monumental in scale.

79

Delft

Of all the main centres of Dutch painting, Delft is the most easily identifiable on grounds of style and quality. The great trio of painters, Carel Fabritius, Pieter de Hooch and Vermeer, span a relatively short period in the 1650s with only Vermeer remaining in the 1660s. Explanation for what might be termed the Delft phenomenon has never been forthcoming. The town did not have any commercial advantages over other main centres – it was essentially a survival from the Middle Ages and retained a Catholic minority to which Vermeer belonged.

There had been some late-medieval painting in Delft and the Master of the Virgo inter Virgines, one of the most refined painters of the late-Gothic tradition in the Northern Netherlands, may have been based there. It could not be said, however, that Delft had the historical continuity of Utrecht or Haarlem and painting activity in the first half of the 17th century was rather below that in many other centres. A major catastrophe occurred in 1654 when a powder magazine blew up destroying a third of the town's inhabited area and killing Carel Fabritius among others. It is likely that there was much destruction of works of art. The devastation is accurately recorded in a painting by Egbert van der Poel of which one of the many versions is in the National Gallery, London.

What sets the great period of painting in Delft apart is its high aesthetic quality. The young Carel Fabritius, for example, rose above anecdote, accurate portraiture and topography and almost all his few surviving pictures break new ground. His elaborate but minuscule *View of Delft* (London, National Gallery) may well have been produced for a peep show, certainly the perspective is unique for an easel painting. The male heads included have a brooding quality suggesting that some, if not all of them, are self-portraits.

Similarly, Pieter de Hooch's courtyard scenes have more than an anecdotal quality. The greatest master of this genre was, of course, Vermeer and much has been written emphasising his uniqueness. He was not especially popular in Delft as he had but few patrons. What is clear, however, is that it was specifically in Delft that his esoteric art could flourish. At the end of his life he painted the *Allegory of the Catholic Faith* (New York, Metropolitan Museum), presumably for a private client. Because of Vermeer's celebrated *View of Delft* (The Hague, Mauritshuis) the topography of Delft is perhaps better-known than that of any other Dutch city. In the true Delft tradition Vermeer was far from accurate and he widened the water considerably for pictorial effect. Indeed, the most accurate view of Delft is by Jan van der Heyden, the Amsterdam artist (Oslo, Nasjonalgalleriet).

A major attraction to Delft artists was the surrounding medieval heritage and the two great Gothic churches, the Oude Kerk and the Nieuwe Kerk (p.109), were painted by several artists. In the early 1650s Houckgeest and Emanuel de Witte described them with a novel and happy fusion of subtle light and complex perspective which were models for later paintings of church interiors. Emanuel de Witte spent much of his later career in Amsterdam to which Pieter de Hooch also migrated. Thus the brief period of artistic experimentation in Delft in the 1650s had far-reaching effects in Amsterdam for the remaining years of the century.

Leonaert Bramer
Delft 1596 – Delft 1674

Recent research has shown that Bramer was one of the leading painters in Delft in the years before Vermeer matured; their careers ran parallel and they died within a year of one another. Bramer is an enigmatic figure for different reasons than Vermeer. Most of Bramer's large-scale works executed in Delft have not survived. Bramer is therefore now known as the painter of a relatively small number of small-scale pictures which are much more international in their outlook than might be expected in Delft in the middle years of the century. Bramer had spent some years before 1625 in Italy and this influence never left him. He reacted to Adam Elsheimer rather than to Caravaggio and like Elsheimer's, many of Bramer's pictures are on a small scale, are executed on copper and are set at night. Bramer also introduced elements of fantasy into his pictures, one of the best examples being the *Scene of Witchcraft* (Bordeaux, Musée des Beaux-Arts).

The question of whether Bramer was influential on Vermeer has been raised but not satisfactorily answered. It is sufficient to note that Vermeer's early pictures show an awareness of Italian sources which may have come via Bramer.

80. Christ before the High Priest Caiaphas
canvas; 71.1 × 100.3 cm
Birmingham City Museums and Art Gallery
This picture is unusually large in scale and ambitious in composition; Bramer's night scenes are often slighter in mood with the figures only sketchily indicated. The artist has used

80

a number of compositional devices to enhance the feeling of drama in this subject, Christ's interrogation by Caiaphas. The figure holding Christ and a further figure on the right are shown in silhouette. Caiaphas, seated, leans forward in an interrogatory position, his finger pointing. These exaggerations are toned down by the use of artificial light largely derived from Adam Elsheimer (*eg Judith and Holofernes*, London, Wellington Museum). In a European context such pictures are more common than is usually supposed and one could point to Claude Vignon in France and Schönfeldt later in Germany as other exponents.

Anthonie Palamedes

Delft 1601 – Amsterdam 1673

Palamedes was the most accomplished painter of middle-class interior scenes. He added elegant figures to the work of other artists including those by Dirck van Delen (p.53). His pictures are remarkably consistent in style and only betray their date by changes in fashion, such as the gradual raising of the height of women's waistlines in the 1630s.

81. Interior with Cavaliers and Ladies
panel; 59.7 × 87.6cm
Nottingham Castle Museum and Art Gallery
The contrast between this and the picture of almost exactly the same subject but of slightly earlier date by Pieter Codde (p.129) is illuminating. The company are better behaved although they are obviously having a good time. There are more indications of luxury. The pictures on the wall have grander frames, the furniture is more impressive and the

81

company enjoy a delicacy – roast swan. There are numerous other small touches for the observant eye ranging from the Delftware vases in imitation of Chinese ware, perched rather precariously on top of the cupboard, to the increased finery of the ladies' dresses.

Pieter de Hooch

Rotterdam 1629 – Amsterdam 1684

Pieter de Hooch had a long career which divides unequally into two parts. During his early period in Delft he was one of the subtlest of the painters of middle-class interiors and city courtyards. More than his contemporary Vermeer of Delft, he epitomised the values of the Dutch Republic. He straightforwardly stated domestic virtue whereas Vermeer almost always proposed a moral message. Contrary to popular perception, de Hooch's Delft pictures are very rare, rarer than the works of Vermeer.

Most of de Hooch's later career was spent in Amsterdam where his style changed dramatically. His technique became more rapid although still careful. The pale tonalities of his Delft period were abandoned and he was more preoccupied with the fall of light within dark interiors. His figures became more elegant and stylised. These pictures, although less appreciated today, conformed much more than his early works to contemporary taste.

82. A Courtyard in Delft at Evening, a Woman spinning

canvas; 69.2 × 53.4cm

Royal Collection, London

Reproduced by gracious permission of Her Majesty The Queen

Pieter de Hooch only painted a handful of courtyard scenes of which this is one of the most atmospheric. This simple genre piece is preoccupied with the unusual and difficult task of portraying the effect of evening light. In the background is the tall tower of the Nieuwe Kerk in Delft (p. 109 for van

Vliet's interior view) and to its right the much lower tower of the Stadhuis. De Hooch's observation ranges from the fall of light on tiles and bricks to the poses and expressions of the two figures. The extreme fineness of the observation can be seen in the irregular application of whitewash to the bricks on the right and in the complex tonal relationships between the silhouettes of the buildings.

82 [colour plate IX]

Johannes Vermeer of Delft
Delft 1632 – Delft 1675

Vermeer only became a household word in the 20th century. Following his death he was utterly neglected and his pictures fetched relatively low prices in 18th-century sales. The revival of his reputation began in 1867 with an article in the *Gazette des Beaux-Arts* by Thoré-Bürger who first identified Vermeer as the painter of a small group of exquisite genre pieces. There has been considerable scholarly enquiry into the artist's background and environment and now a good deal more is known about the artistic scene in Delft in the middle years of the century. There has been no drastic reassessment of his pictures although a number of them have come under increasing scrutiny because of their damaged state.

Vermeer's painstaking technique changed during his career as he applied paint in a more and more transparent and enamel-like manner. It is likely that Vermeer used an optical aid to achieve the closed perspective of his pictures and such an instrument would also have had the effect of concentrating the lighting – hence the tiny dots or pin points of light which are such a characteristic of his work. Most of Vermeer's genre pieces have some obvious moral, such as *The Procuress* (Dresden, Gemäldegalerie) or can represent a less obvious religious allegory, such as the *Woman with Scales* (Washington, National Gallery). He also painted a few pure genre scenes such as *Maidservant pouring Milk* (Amsterdam, Rijksmuseum).

83 [colour plate XXV]

83. Young Lady at a Virginal
canvas; 51.5 × 45.3 cm
National Gallery, London
Reproduced by courtesy of the Trustees
This picture is overshadowed in the National Gallery by the lighter, more brilliantly lit *Lady Standing at the Virginals* with which it is sometimes paired even though they are painted in rather different styles. This painting is a late work, almost certainly from the last five years of Vermeer's life, when he was changing his style to accommodate increasingly Baroque and French-inspired trends. Technically the picture

is curiously uneven; the cello and virginals are carefully painted using minute gradations of tone, while the blue of the woman's dress is metallic in feeling and is perhaps unfinished. The same brittle surface is also found in *The Guitar Player* (London, Kenwood) and it may be that this is a characteristic of Vermeer's last paintings as exemplified by the *Allegory of the Catholic Faith* (New York, Metropolitan Museum).

The meaning of the picture has been much debated around the contrast between the lady innocently making music and the painting in the background of a *Procuress* by the earlier Dutch artist Baburen (a version of which is in Boston, Massachusetts). The picture can be read as a simple genre piece accidentally including an example of the Caravaggesque Utrecht school in the background, or as an allegory of Profane (seated lady) and Sacred (standing lady at virginals) Love. The woman looking out, slightly quizzically, at the spectator, creates a deeply intimate mood, and such a private art was out of tune with the times. It is easy to see why, in his last years, Vermeer had difficulty in supporting himself and his large family.

Hendrick Cornelis van Vliet

Delft 1611/12 – Delft 1675

Most of van Vliet's pictures are church interiors and the majority of these interiors represent the large medieval churches of Delft, the Oude Kerk and Nieuwe Kerk. Van Vliet lacked the cool detachment of Saenredam or the passion for light, shadow and atmosphere found in the best pictures of Emanuel de Witte. Instead his church interiors tend to be anecdotal in their approach and descriptive in their intent. The artist paints his hatchments and tombs as identifiable monuments rather than as compositional elements for purely artistic ends. No doubt local art collectors in Delft wanted records of the interior of their two great churches.

Van Vliet was also a portrait painter of merit although there is still some confusion between his portraits and those of his father Willem van Vliet.

84. Interior of the Nieuwe Kerk at Delft, 1667
canvas; 127 × 85.5 cm
Liverpool Royal Institution, on loan to the National Museums on Merseyside, Liverpool City Council and the Governors of the Liverpool Institute
The Nieuwe Kerk at Delft contains the only shrine of the Dutch Republic – the tomb of its founder, William the Silent. The Dutch had few heroes as their history before the 17th century had been one of occupation by authorities anxious to tax their growing wealth. The Nieuwe Kerk, therefore, became the Dutch Valhalla and as such was painted many times by most of the church interior specialist painters. In no other Dutch church is a tomb placed so prominently and, but for the Reformation, it would have stood before the high altar.

84 [colour plate XXIV]

This is one of van Vliet's most successful compositions, the complex perspective painted with cool clarity. The contrast to the contemplative quality of Saenredam could not be greater as Saenredam had no interest in the incidental qualities of his interiors and, significantly, he never painted a Delft church even though he travelled much greater distances from Haarlem where he lived. Van Vliet's picture gives an accurate contemporary view of a Dutch church with armorial hatchments, flags and with a grave being dug.

85. A Woman reading
metal; 22.9 × 16.7 cm
Cheltenham Art Gallery
The attribution of this picture to van Vliet is traditional and recent research on it has not been able to provide a convincing alternative. The painting certainly fits the context of Delft in mid-century when that city, despite the calamitous explosion of the powder magazine in 1654, was in the forefront of artis-

85

86

tic activity. The tenderness and intimacy of this small-scale genre piece, if not its style, is reminiscent of Vermeer himself, but the absence of a date does not allow any precise relationship to be established.

Willem van Aelst

Delft 1627 – Amsterdam *c.*1683 ?

Van Aelst gained the distinction of Medici patronage in Florence and a number of his elaborate hunting pieces remain in the Pitti and Uffizi Galleries there. He was also a specialist flower painter of highly refined pictures with dark backgrounds and Baroque compositions first produced by Jan Davidsz. de Heem. Van Aelst's hunting pieces are more original. In common with so many painters working in the second half of the century, he paid great attention to the surface texture of each object in a picture, sometimes at the expense of tonal unity.

86. Still-Life with Dead Game, 1673
canvas; 96.5 × 76.2 cm
Leeds City Art Galleries

The essence of such a picture as this is illusion – a three-dimensional effect close to *trompe l'œil*. This is enhanced by the disconcerting placing of the gun on the left, a feature that can also be found in Jan van der Heyden's rare still-lifes. The feathers, metal and cloth are painted with equal skill and it is easy to see how such painting captivated Italian patrons in the absence of any similar paintings by Italian artists.

Jan Denysz.

working Delft *c.*1643/49

Denysz.'s few surviving pictures continue the style perfected by van Aelst (p.110) in the 1660s and do not reflect the changes of taste that affected still-life and flower painting in the last quarter of the century.

87. A Glass Vase of Flowers
canvas; 88.2 × 69.2 cm
The Syndics of the Fitzwilliam Museum, Cambridge
This is one of the more ambitious works by Denysz. whose pictures are especially rare. In concept it is much indebted to the artist's master, Willem van Aelst, although the latter usually worked on a rather smaller scale. The flowers are

87

roses, tulips and poppies with an iris and columbine. All these flowers bloom in the early summer thus giving the picture a seasonal feel absent when flowers from all seasons are mixed into magnificent artificial bouquets.

Adam Pijnacker

Pijnacker 1621 – Amsterdam 1673

Pijnacker was the last of the great Italianising landscapists and made a distinct contribution to the genre at a relatively late date as, typically, the half-century after 1650 was to see an ever more meticulous repetition of the old models (established by Jan Both and Poelenburgh in particular). Pijnacker took the standard, mountainous, wooded landscape, established by Jan Both about 1640, and gave it his own slightly surreal interpretation. Pijnacker's trees are a little more twisted than nature usually allows and his foreground vegetation is a little exaggerated both in form and colour. His skies take on a special porcelain-like blue and his yellow light is often a little too yellow. His pictures, especially on an ambitious scale, enter the realm of the imagination rather than realism.

88. Mountainous wooded Landscape
canvas; 90 × 81.2 cm
University of Edinburgh (Torrie Collection)
On superficial inspection this picture is a stereotyped Italianate landscape in the tradition of Jan Both (p.50) who initiated this type of composition and lighting effect. A closer look reveals an artificiality based on the imagination rather than observation. The relationships between the trees, water and hills are not entirely convincing and, in the case of the large central tree, seem out of scale. The very artificiality of this brilliantly-coloured stage scenery gives Pijnacker a status greater than is generally appreciated – he is not, for example, represented in the National Gallery, London.

88 [colour plate XVII]

Rotterdam

The size of the medieval St Laurenskerk in Rotterdam (rebuilt after destruction in the Second World War) indicates a reasonable level of prosperity in the late Middle Ages but Rotterdam's prosperity was always outstripped by that of Dordrecht to the south and Delft to the north. In the 17th century there was little indication that the town was to become the largest Dutch port in subsequent centuries.

It cannot be said, however, that artistic activity languished – the reverse seems to have been the case as it was stimulated by the proximity of Delft which lies just a few miles to the north. There was artistic activity in Rotterdam throughout the century, although it seems to have remained at a fairly static level without dramatic increase or falling off.

A few painters of distinction originated from Rotterdam, including Emanuel de Witte although he worked primarily in Delft and Amsterdam. There is no specifically identifiable Rotterdam style and Rotterdam artists generally depended on Delft. There was no painter as in Haarlem or Utrecht who produed a succession of landscapes reflecting local topography. The St Laurenskerk, especially its interior, was favoured by the Middelburg painter Daniel de Blieck but there is a conspicuous lack of picturesque views of the town.

Instead the emphasis seems to have been on genre painting which almost all the painters of real distinction practised. The earliest and one of the best was Willem Buytewech from whose hand only a handful of works survive. These are robust scenes of well-dressed cavaliers drinking in interiors, with maps and pictures on the wall. He had no talented successor in Rotterdam and the pattern remained unchanged.

Typically, Rotterdam painters matured under Delft influence and failed to establish any tradition of their own. But Rotterdam did produce some interesting figures, such as the recently rediscovered Duifhuyzen (p.113) and the quirky Colonia (p.116) who spent the second half of his career in England.

Among the best of Rotterdam painters was Ochtervelt (p.116), the only Dutch painter to understand and continue Vermeer's tradition of genre painting. At the very end of the century, at a time when Rotterdam's relative prosperity was increasing, Adriaen van der Werff (p.120) was the leading painter active in the city despite the fact that he spent part of the year on contract to the Elector Palatine at Düsseldorf. Van der Werff gained an international reputation in his lifetime even though his compositions were based on previous Dutch or French models. His internationalism shows how Rotterdam had developed away from its isolated position at the beginning of the century.

Hendrick Martensz. Sorgh
Rotterdam 1610/11 – Rotterdam 1670

Sorgh is usually classed as a minor genre painter of little significance outside the context of his native Rotterdam. In fact he was a much more varied painter than this and produced competent if not innovative seascapes in the monochrome tradition and genre pieces which sometimes contained religious subjects (see below). In general tonality the genre pieces tend towards a brownish-grey characteristic of the Rotterdam genre painter Cornelis Saftleven and of those Haarlem genre painters who worked under the influence of Adriaen van Ostade.

89. Christ in the House of Martha and Mary, 1645
panel; 39.3 × 50.8 cm
Cheltenham Art Gallery
Contrary to popular estimation a very high proportion of Dutch painters executed religious works at some point in their careers even though no one artist painted religious pictures exclusively. This work is important because it is dated and can, therefore, be proved to be at least a decade earlier than Vermeer's celebrated treatment of the same subject (Edinburgh, National Gallery of Scotland). Even though there is no stylistic similarity between the Sorgh and the Vermeer, this picture shows that the subject was an established one and that Vermeer's originality was in his interpretations of the subject rather than in his choice of it. In the Sorgh, the subject is treated as genre with the gesture of reproach between Martha and Mary tying the two halves of the composition together. There can be ambiguity about such a religious subject when the figures are not in historical costume – a famous example is Rembrandt's *The Jewish Bride* (Amsterdam, Rijksmuseum). But there is no ambiguity here about the subject as Christ is clearly identifiable by his clothes and the radiance emanating from the back of his head.

Pieter Jacobsz. Duifhuyzen
Rotterdam 1608 – Rotterdam 1677

Duifhuyzen's few surviving pictures have only been identified recently by Willem L van de Watering. Duifhuyzen spent his career in Rotterdam which had a surprising number of artists active in it given the proximity of Delft or the more important Dordrecht which lies to the south. The influence of David Teniers

89

is strong in Duifhuyzen as it is in other Rotterdam artists such as Arent Diepraam. This might be explained by nearness to the Flemish border.

90. The Lace Maker
panel; 34 × 26 cm
Private Collection
Lace makers are common enough in Dutch painting of the period and are almost over-familiar through Vermeer's brilliant small picture of *The Lace Maker* (Paris, Louvre). In this instance, however, a soldier's breastplate, sword and helmet lie beside the seated woman who wears a slightly quizzical expression suggesting a romantic interpretation, the lady's thoughts for her absent cavalier. Such a level of intimacy is rare among minor genre painters who usually preferred a more obvious treatment of their subject. On the wall, in a standard dark Dutch frame, is a realistic landscape with trees, clouds and figures.

Hendrick de Meyer
Rotterdam *c.*1627 – Rotterdam *c.*1690

Hendrick de Meyer was a versatile artist whose pictures would be difficult to identify without signatures. The likely reason for this is that he was working in the then relatively small town of Rotterdam where there were fewer specialists. He would satisfy a broader demand imitating with some skill the work of artists as diverse as Jan van Goyen and Aelbert Cuyp. His work has been confused in the past with both these artists. The artist's best pictures are skating scenes with animated figures.

91. Travellers outside an Inn, 1648
panel; 97.8 × 86.3 cm
Essex County Council: Chelmsford Shire Hall
The scene records the arrival (or departure) of an important

90

person at an elaborately picturesque inn. Varnish obscures a strong grey-blue sky. This picture is unusually ambitious for de Meyer who normally worked on a smaller scale and preferred winter scenes.

91

Jacob Ochtervelt

working Rotterdam *c.*1652-1712

Ochtervelt represents the closing phase of Dutch 17th-century genre painting when powers of invention were beginning to wane and skill was more highly prized by collectors. Ochtervelt belongs to a generation when these opposing factors, inventiveness versus skill, were working against one another. Ochtervelt's pictures are based in some respect on what had gone before, which gives them an over-familiar look, however skilfully they are painted. His elegant genre scenes bring together a variety of influences from Metsu, Terborch and, surprisingly, Vermeer of Delft (p.108). The first part of his career was spent in Rotterdam before a move to Amsterdam in 1674 where he remained.

92. The Music Lesson
canvas; 76.7 × 78.1 cm
On the lid of the spinet is inscribed the motto: *Musica Laborum Dulce Levamen*
Birmingham City Museums and Art Gallery
Despite Ochtervelt's limitations in comparison with Terborch and Metsu, this painting is outstanding and an example of a painter outside the mainstream who could produce an occasional masterpiece. The theme of the music lesson occurs first around 1650 in famous examples by Metsu (London, National Gallery) and Vermeer (Boston, Gardner Museum, and Windsor Castle, Royal Collection). In all these pictures by other artists there is an element of mystery to the music makers. The man in the shadows may be instructor or seducer, or both. The clue in this case is the expression of the maid's animated face which shows an awareness of the situation not betrayed by the demure look of the lady of quality who is playing the spinet. Ochtervelt became old-fashioned after 1670 in contrast to the late work of Vermeer (*Young Lady at a Virginal*, p.108), where the artist has progressed from the style he favoured in the 1660s to the 'modern' approach of the 1670s, taking into account French fashions and an increased awareness of classical mythology and moral allegory.

92

Adam Colonia

Rotterdam 1634 – London 1685

Colonia spent the greater part of his career in England where he seems to have been successful. His early style

93

in his years in Rotterdam was, as might be expected, somewhat eclectic, the chief influences coming from Utrecht as happened with other Rotterdam painters such as Volmarijn. Colonia was essentially a landscapist but filled his pictures with lively figures. His style tends to be rather coarse, especially in his later pictures executed in England. The two pictures at Dulwich are good examples of his work and it is traditionally held that the four copies after Bassano in the Dulwich Collection were executed by Colonia. In any case, the Venetian landscapists, and especially the Bassano family, influenced Colonia's work.

93. Noah leaving the Ark
canvas; 90.5 × 94.6 cm
Bolton Museum and Art Gallery

94

It is rare to show the animals leaving the ark rather than entering it. In this amusing picture the artist has leaned heavily on Utrecht painters for his inspiration. The Italianate landscape is derived from Jan Both and the *mêlée* of animals from Roelant Savery. The humour lies in the human expressions of the animals. The *finesse* of this picture is unusual for Colonia who was generally much coarser in his handling of paint. Indeed, it may be taken to be one of the artist's best surviving pictures.

Abraham Hondius

Rotterdam *c.*1625/30 – London 1691/95

Hondius occupies an ambivalent position in the appreciation of Dutch 17th-century painting because the later part of his career was spent in England and his subject-matter has never endeared itself to modern taste. He specialised in hunting pieces, not the elegant arrangements of a Jan Weenix but raw violent scenes where animals tear each other apart watched over by the hunter.

94. The Wild Boar Hunt
canvas; 68.6 × 82.6 cm
Wolverhampton Art Gallery
Two dogs attack a wild boar, one dog has been hurled ignominiously to the ground and the other snarls in rage at the beleaguered animal protecting its young. More dogs follow up in the background. For sheer aggressive violence few Dutch pictures of the time match this work. This corrects a view of the Dutch 17th century as one of untroubled peasant order and bourgeois prosperity interspersed with a little mis-

95

behaviour. It is not possible to tell on stylistic grounds whether or not the picture was executed in England. Indeed, in most cases concerning Dutch artists, this can only be done through documentation, as with the pictures in the Royal Collection, or because a picture bears a date or because it represents a British subject (*eg The Dutch burning the English Fleet at Chatham* by Schellincks, p.146).

Adriaen van der Werff
Kralingen 1659 – Rotterdam 1722

There has been a recent revival of interest in Adriaen van der Werff after a century of neglect. When Houbraken published his biography of Dutch painters in 1726, he placed van der Werff above all other Dutch painters of the 17th century. Certainly the artist had achieved an international reputation rare in his time. He was contracted out to Johann Wilhelm the Elector Palatine and was required to work in Düsseldorf for a specific part of each year. Many of the paintings he executed for the Elector are now at Schloss Schleissheim, just outside Munich. Van der Werff's style was meticulous to the point of exaggeration and in his enamel-like paintings tone values are frequently abandoned in favour of surface smoothness. His subject-matter was inventive and, apart from portraits, he executed a number of complex mythological and religious pictures which betray both French and Italian influence.

95. Portrait of a Woman
canvas; 47.6 × 39 cm
Glasgow Art Gallery and Museum
This picture is an excellent example of late-17th-century Dutch portraiture as it differed from the contemporary conventions of Lely and Kneller in England or of the Mignard/Bourdon tradition in France. The sitter has been given an informal sumptuousness (their day-to-day dress would have been much stiffer and more formal) and the flesh has a marble-like clarity dramatically different from the robust pink tones of earlier Dutch portraiture. There is an element of symbolism in the picture, the two Cupids at the fountain symbolising love, and the man in the background adopts an attitude associated with Pan. The studied elegance and careful craftsmanship used in pictures of this type did not long remain fashionable because van der Werff's followers lacked his ability.

96 [colour plate XXXI]

96. St Margaret
panel; 43.2 × 31 cm
Gloucester City Museums
Part of van der Werff's international reputation rested on the fact that his subject-matter had cosmopolitan appeal in the early-18th century. It is likely that this painting belonged to Marguerite Louise d'Orléans (1645 - 1721). As is usual with van der Werff, the surface is polished to resemble enamel rather than oil paint. In this period innovation was frowned upon and this *St Margaret*, recently cleaned for exhibition, reveals just how reliant van der Werff had become on an existing tradition. The large work by Nicolas Poussin of the same subject (Turin, Galleria Sabauda) immeditely comes to mind as the source for this picture. In the apocryphal story, St Margaret was swallowed by a dragon from which she escaped when it burst!

Dordrecht

Dordrecht, commonly known as 'Dort' to the English, was a significant port in the Middle Ages owing to its strategic position on one of the mouths of the Rhine – the Maas. The medieval walled town was extensive and is still dominated by the unfinished late Gothic tower of the Grote Kerk. This tower, so often seen across the water, was a favourite subject for painters and in particular to Jan van Goyen and Aelbert Cuyp (p.123).

Apart from Middelburg in Zeeland, Dordrecht was the most southerly of the main Dutch towns and might, therefore, have been isolated from the main centres of activity. The reverse appears to have been the case because of the number of Dordrecht painters who were aware of what was going on in Amsterdam. Painting activity throughout the whole century was dominated by the Cuyp family, at first as portraitists and later as genre and religious painters (p.122). Aelbert Cuyp (p.122) proved to be an extremely influential painter later in the century (*eg* upon Abraham Calraet) and throughout the 18th century when his pastoral pictures, landscapes with cows bathed in a golden glow, were both imitated and forged.

Besides the Dordrecht style epitomised by the Cuyp family was another strong influence, which is often overlooked, that might loosely be termed Rembrandtism. Three Rembrandt-trained artists came to Dordrecht: Nicolaes Maes, who changed his style radically; Samuel van Hoogstraten, who was too individual to succumb to Rembrandt for too long; and Aert de Gelder (p.125), who imitated Rembrandt's late manner for almost fifty years after his death. The activity of these three painters shows that Dordrecht clients wanted up-to-date pictures, especially in the second half of the century. Dordrecht, like near-by Rotterdam, avoided the economic decline that affected some other Dutch centres and was able to sustain a thriving artistic life.

Dordrecht apparently had a distinct preference for a certain type of artistic style rather than for a broad representation of the different genres. No significant still-life or genre painters worked successfully as specialists in Dordrecht although most artists active there tried their hand at a variety of subjects. A significant example of this modification to suit local needs is found in the Dordrecht work of Maes (p.124) who abandoned his anecdotal Amsterdam genre style in favour of compositions with a distinctly local flavour, such as portraits with the silhouette of the Grote Kerk in the background.

The sentimental affection in which views of Dordrecht have been held in the past is typified by Aelbert Cuyp's large-scale cow piece in the National Gallery, London, affectionately known as '*The Large Dort*'.

Benjamin Gerritsz. Cuyp
Dordrecht 1612 – Dordrecht 1652

Benjamin Gerritsz. Cuyp was the uncle of the celebrated Aelbert Cuyp (p.122), a member of a family of painters practising in Dordrecht since the end of the 16th century. Indeed, the history of painting in Dordrecht in the first half of the 17th century is essentially that of the Cuyp family even though they worked in styles which were often widely divergent from one another. Throughout his career he used great fluidity of handling and on panel his brushwork flows almost too easily, which imparts a sketchiness to his figures and backgrounds. Many of his compositions are dramatic, whether biblical scenes such as the Annunciation to the Shepherds or the Nativity, or peasant brawls and battle scenes. Most of his genres are represented in the Dordrechts Museum at Dordrecht.

97. Peasant Brawl
panel; 29.2 × 36.8 cm
Trustees of the Holburne Museum, Bath
In its present state this picture is almost monochrome, although the 1936 Museum Catalogue mentions touches of colour and typically Cuyp enlivened his mainly brown and ochre palette with small patches of more intense colour.

Scenes of the poor brawling are very common in Dutch painting and are taken by some to be the epitome of it. The sternest chronicler of the foibles of the poor was van de Venne (p.52) and Benjamin Gerritsz. Cuyp never approached the latter's irony. This is a less cruel view of the miseries and drolleries of the poor and the unseemliness of the squabble may raise a smile even though blood has been drawn. This picture thus stands mid-way between van de Venne and the almost elegant interpretations of Adriaen van Ostade who illustrated the lives of the poor with refined colour and technique and without any strong moral overtone.

98. The Adoration of the Shepherds
panel; 110 × 84 cm
Kilmarnock and Loudoun District Museums, Dick Institute, Kilmarnock
Even though this is a religious subject, the artist's style is instantly recognisable from that of the peasant scene at Bath (p.122). The artist owes a debt to the early work of Rembrandt, especially to those pictures painted in Leiden before 1631. The piling-up of the figures and even the facial types betray this influence. As in almost all Rembrandt's religious work,

97

98

the Bible story is told with maximum simplicity and without the sentiment and charm typical of both the Mannerists and Caravaggesques. In order to increase the realistic effect the artist has added to the usual number of three shepherds.

Aelbert Cuyp
Dordrecht 1620 – Dordrecht 1691

The reputation and achievements of Aelbert Cuyp parallel those of Hobbema – scant attention paid in the artist's lifetime, conspicuous neglect for the hundred years or so after, and rising interest from the mid-18th century charted through increasing prices in the salerooms. The Napoleonic era and the decades following saw a meteoric rise in both artists' reputations with a consequent confusion over attribution. The last hundred years has seen a gradual but not altogether successful attempt to redefine their status. Cuyp appealed both to early Victorian Romantic taste and to later Victorian opulent taste. However, only a part of Cuyp's work has attracted collectors and public – cows reclining by or standing in water bathed in golden light has subsequently become the cliché.

Cuyp was one of the most various painters of his time and executed portraits, still-life pictures, landscapes, sea pieces and variations of these types, such as equestrian pieces set in landscape. Even the most recent book on Cuyp steadfastly ignores Cuyp's breadth and concentrates on him as a phenomenon in the history of taste and more specifically in the history of taste in landscape painting. Of all the Dutch Italianate painters (and only in some respects does he fall into this category) Cuyp was the one who understood best the fall of light.

99. View of Dordrecht, Evening
canvas; 97.8 × 138.5 cm
The Iveagh Bequest, Kenwood, London (English Heritage)
Although this picture is a second version of Cuyp's greatest picture (at Ascott), it exists in its own right as one of the artist's most successful works. On a golden evening in summer, the sun strikes the west face of the tower of Dordrecht's unfinished Gothic Grote Kerk as the shadows stretch out over the calm water. Cuyp had few equals in creating balance, harmony and atmosphere and this picture demonstrates his skill in subtly distributing the separate elements – ships, figures, sky, water and the fall of light.

100. River Scene with Cows near Vianen
panel; 38.7 × 54.4 cm
Private Collection, on loan to Birmingham Museums and Art Gallery
Cuyp has handled the light in this picture with characteristic subtlety. The effect is one of evening with the subdued golden glow from a sun low in the sky, a moment perhaps between rain showers. Herdsman and cow are silhouetted against a low horizon as in nature. Indeed, in such pictures

99 [colour plate XI]

Cuyp is far more naturalistic than is usually supposed. Beyond we see some of the principal buildings of a town. The mood is tranquil and detached. Stephen Reiss has suggested that the town may be Vianen just south of Utrecht and proposed a date in the mid-1640s. The identification is confirmed by a contemporary and slightly different view of the town by Salomon van Ruysdael (p.92). The picture is Reiss, no.26 and was exhibited at the National Gallery, *Aelbert Cuyp in British Collections*, 1973, no.4.

Nicolaes Maes
Dordrecht 1634 – Amsterdam 1693

Maes is an enigmatic painter as his reputation rests on a few superlative genre paintings executed under the influence of Rembrandt's studio while most of his surviving pictures are portraits, generally small in scale, with great attention to surface texture rather than detail. He worked in Rembrandt's studio as a pupil until the early 1650s and then returned to Dordrecht. He is said to have gone to Antwerp *c.*1660 and stayed there for five years. Thereafter most of his career was spent in Amsterdam. It is likely that the changes in the artist's style and subject-matter reflect more or less accurately these moves. A few early religious works are eclectic in style but his genre pictures are highly original and his eavesdropping housemaids, for instance, are both convincing and 'true to life', unlike those set in the elegant world of Metsu (p.60), Terborch (p.72) or Pieter de Hooch (p.107). Maes' portraits, on the other hand, lack this strong sense of individuality and reflect the fashionable ideals of the bourgeoisie in the last third of the century.

100

101

101. A Boy with his Dog, 1662
panel; 36.8 × 45.7 cm
The Royal Pavilion, Art Gallery and Museums, Brighton
This picture marks a transition in Maes' subject-matter from genre to portraiture. It is likely that, given the immense competition in genre painting, and Maes was more subtle and inventive than most, the artist found portraiture more lucrative. This example of a sitter in the landscape is of a type quite often found in Dordrecht in pictures by members of the Cuyp family. The clearly recognisable silhouette of the Grote Kerk at Dordrecht can also be seen in the background of Aelbert Cuyp's great view of Dordrecht (p. 122). Unusually for Maes the treatment of the whole landscape is strongly reminiscent of Cuyp, which is a clear indication of the strength of the tradition established by that family of painters in Dordrecht.

102. A young Gentleman
canvas; 42 × 29.2 cm
Trustees of the Holburne Museum, Bath
This is a typical example of Maes' portrait style from the latter part of his career and recent cleaning has brought out the intensity of the colour often found in the artist's later works. The identification of the sitter as one of the sons of the celebrated Dutch Admiral de Ruyter has not been proved. The relatively late date of the picture is indicated by the elaboration of the clothes and the length of the hair. The bourgeois

102

103

austerity of the middle years of the century had been abandoned in the face of the influx of French fashions after the French invasion of 1672.

Aert de Gelder

Dordrecht 1645 – Dordrecht 1727

Although correctly classified as one of Rembrandt's pupils, de Gelder is the most individualistic of all such pupils and the one who carried the Rembrandtesque tradition to the end of the first quarter of the 18th century – a time when the wheel of taste had come full circle and Rembrandt's pictures were beginning to be appreciated again. De Gelder's technique was one of encrusted paint shot with different and unexpected colours. This gives his pictures a vibrancy akin to the textures found in Rembrandt's late works as in *The Jewish Bride* (Amsterdam, Rijksmuseum). His style developed little during a career spanning some fifty years and so the dating of his pictures is problematical. It is now difficult to understand how de Gelder's pictures could have been confused with those of Rembrandt. The rather dark *Jacob's Ladder* in the Dulwich Gallery was thought to be by Rembrandt in the 19th century when it was one of the most popular pictures there.

103. Ahasuerus and Haman
canvas; 138.5 × 116.8 cm
Trustees of the Barber Institute of Fine Arts, University of Birmingham
This is one of Aert de Gelder's most Rembrandtesque pictures, for instance the brooding quality, and it probably dates from an early stage in de Gelder's career. However, neither of Rembrandt's two versions of the subject (Moscow, Pushkin Museum, and Leningrad, Hermitage Museum) select this particular moment when Haman gives false counsel to the suspicious King Ahasuerus. The story of Esther's deliverance of the Jews from the enmity of Haman during the Babylonian captivity was evidently popular at the time both on stage and in pictures, Jan Steen as well as Rembrandt illustrating it.

As a description of human expression the picture is effective, but the debt to Rembrandt prevents us from seeing this as a new invention. Such intense and heavily textured pictures were often attributed to Rembrandt, especially in the 18th century when false Rembrandt signatures were often added to them.

Amsterdam

Amsterdam was one of the most cosmopolitan cities of its age, pre-eminent in Northern Europe from the middle of the 17th century as a commercial port and trading centre. The town hall, rebuilt following a fire, was, for its time, of prodigious size. (Since 1815 it has been the Dutch Royal Palace, its original function long forgotten and major parts of its decoration by Rembrandt and others no longer *in situ*.) No other Dutch city was open to such a wide variety of foreign cultural influences. Collectors such as Rembrandt could acquire Persian miniatures as well as more conventional objects for their collections. As the art market in Amsterdam developed, artists had the opportunity of seeing works of the Italian Renaissance without travelling to Italy and Rembrandt, for example, made drawings of Italian pictures passing through the trade. By comparison, therefore, a near-by city like Haarlem could remain relatively insular, which explains the consistency of approach of Haarlem artists.

Amsterdam's medieval and 16th-century past was relatively modest beside that of Leiden, Utrecht, Haarlem or even Delft. This is borne out by the scale of the two medieval churches which at the time had to serve the entire population. The 17th-century expansion of Amsterdam was prodigious; the medieval town had only been a few hundred yards across and the area more than quadrupled when laid out on a system of concentric canals. Significantly all the other centres kept more or less to their medieval boundaries siting within them new churches of relatively modest dimensions (*eg* Haarlem and Rotterdam). In Amsterdam there were several large new churches throughout the city which, with the exception of the assiduous Jan van der Heyden, did not attract much interest from the topographical artist. The topography of Amsterdam was generally ignored by artists in the first half of the century too, Saenredam's exquisite small-scale picture of the medieval town hall being the exception (Amsterdam, Rijksmuseum). All this changed in the 1660s with the building of the new town hall and the Dam Square which became a favourite subject for Jan van der Heyden and others.

In contrast to the artistic cohesion of Haarlem, Utrecht, Leiden and Delft, Amsterdam is remarkable for its diversity. The city supported by far the largest number of painters at any one time from about 1640 onwards and as a result there is no specific Amsterdam style. Styles were brought to Amsterdam from other centres fully-fledged and existed side by side in fierce competition. From *c.*1660 onwards Jacob van Ruisdael was based in Amsterdam having moved from his native Haarlem. Metsu came from Leiden and Pieter de Hooch from Delft. Thus genre painting was dominated by two artists who came from specific local traditions and landscape painting was dominated by Ruisdael (even though most of his imitators remained in Haarlem).

The merchant classes were the chief buyers of paintings as official commissions from the municipal authorities were few. More than in any other centre painters had to satisfy the current trends, hence the change of emphasis in both subject-matter and style from decade to decade.

There is nothing distinctive about the development of Amsterdam painting up to *c.*1630. The leading painter in the 1620s was Pieter Lastman to whom the young Rembrandt was briefly apprenticed. Lastman was the chief exponent of a homespun version of Italian art, a type of painting that has recently been dubbed Pre-Rembrandtist.

It is obvious, with hindsight, that to young painters wishing to make their careers outside the confines of their local milieu, Amsterdam offered considerable attractions. An analysis of Rembrandt's early career bears this out. He had been highly successful in Leiden, painting small genre and history pieces, but as soon as he arrived in Amsterdam from the end of 1631 he increased the scale of his pictures significantly and began to receive many portrait commissions from the merchant classes. The famous *Anatomy Lesson of Dr Tulp* (The Hague, Mauritshuis) of 1632 was painted immediately after Rembrandt's arrival in Amsterdam. The 1630s were his most prolific and successful period as far as his merchant patrons were concerned and from then on competition increased, ironically from his own pupils such as Ferdinand Bol and Govaert Flinck, as his style began to develop away from the fashionable norm.

There was a gradual but perceptible increase in the value placed upon detail and artists who laboured long over their pictures, however small, were more likely to be well rewarded by patrons and collectors than those who concentrated on broad brushwork and atmosphere. Significantly, at the end of his career, for the important commission of *The Syndics of the Amsterdam Clothworkers Guild* (Amsterdam, Rijksmuseum), Rembrandt modified his late style with tighter control of drawing and texture.

Part of this stylistic change can be attributed directly to the influence of commerce. Pictures, especially small ones, were used as a kind of currency and those that could be easily judged on grounds of sheer mechanical skill were more relevant to buyers who were not connoisseurs of art. More than in any other centre, with the possible exception of Leiden, attention to detail became dominant, for example among the later flower painters such as Jacob van Walscapelle (p.150). It certainly is the strongest characteristic of the brilliant Jan van der Heyden (pp.150f).

Unusually the different genres were equally balanced in Amsterdam. Portraiture continued strongly from the first half of the century (see, for example, several group portraits in the Amsterdams Historisch Museum). Landscape was dominated by country scenes which were especially popular in the 1660s to judge by the high productivity of Aert van der Neer (p.140f) and Hobbema (p.142f). History painting, much of it large-scale, was the speciality of Rembrandt and his pupils. It is difficult to imagine where all the large pictures were placed; most of the backgrounds to genre pieces show how pictures were hung and they usually appear rather small in scale (the exception here is the Utrecht artist Baburen's *Procuress* in the background to Vermeer's *Young Lady at a Virginal* (p.108)).

A history of painting in Amsterdam in the 17th century remains to be written. It would reveal that, despite the vibrancy and consistency of the other main art centres, Amsterdam remained the hub of Dutch painting from *c.*1630 until the end of the century.

Amsterdam school *c.*1600

104. Preparations for a Feast

canvas; 93.5 × 169.5 cm
Birmingham City Museums and Art Gallery
This ambitious picture has attracted some attention from scholars concerning its attribution and interpretation. At first glance it is a simple kitchen scene in the tradition of the Antwerp painter Pieter Aertsen (who spent part of his career in Amsterdam), to whom this picture was long attributed even though it is clearly not much earlier than *c.*1600. The table in the background laid for a meal has been interpreted as representing the Last Supper and many of these early kitchen scenes do include small religious scenes in the background.

The search for an author of this picture must concentrate on Aertsen's Amsterdam pupil Pieter Pietersz. who died in 1603 and who continued Aertsen's style and subject-matter, albeit in a less ambitious format. This picture thus represents

104 [colour plate I]

the end of the 16th-century tradition but also the beginning of a new one. There is a delight in the kitchen utensils and food which looks forward to the extraordinary development of still-life painting, especially in Amsterdam and which culminated in the luxurious banquet pieces of Abraham van Beyeren (p.139).

Bartholomeus Breenbergh
Deventer 1599 – Amsterdam 1657

Breenbergh was the most sensitive of the Dutch painters who went to Italy to specialise in landscape. His career divides into two very distinct phases. He spent the 1620s and early 1630s in Rome where he painted landscapes; the rest of his career was spent in Amsterdam where he specialised in histories and mythologies.

His Italianate landscapes from the first part of his career are usually small in scale and cool in tone. They capture with a crystalline clarity the early morning light of the Roman Campagna and usually lack the more Romantic approach of his contemporary Cornelis van Poelenburgh (p.49). Even so, until recently, the work of the two artists has been confused.

Breenbergh's Amsterdam pictures are different in character, lighting and scale and hark back to an earlier generation, that of the so-called Amsterdam Pre-Rembrandtists (the Pynas brothers, Uyttenbroeck and Moeyaert) not illustrated here. Breenbergh seems to have been unaffected by the great stylistic changes which took place in Amsterdam around 1640 caused by the influence of the mature Rembrandt and his pupils.

105. Peasants and Goats in an Italian Landscape

metal; 12.7 × 16.5 cm
Leeds City Art Galleries
It is not often realised that the first generation of Dutch land-

scape painters working in Italy itself was essentially realist. This is especially true of Poelenburgh and Breenbergh. Their small-scale and minutely-detailed landscapes seem to record a precise location, probably in the environs of Rome. The fact that this picture is painted on copper – a support favoured more by the Flemish than the Dutch – enhances the clear hard detail of the scene. Such precision is later found in the three small-scale circular landscapes painted by Ingres in his early years in Rome.

105

106. Landscape with Amaryllis crowning Myrtillo
canvas; 76.8 × 99.7 cm
Bowes Museum, Barnard Castle, Co. Durham
Dutch artists turned to literary and mythological sources quite often and patrons evidently enjoyed literary or historical allusions in their pictures as a contrast to low-life genre. The subject of this picture, taken from a then popular Italian play *Il pastor fido*, is sexually ambiguous.

The moment depicted is the successful result of a kissing contest. Myrtillo, dressed as a woman, is crowned with a garland of flowers by Amaryllis, the girl who is reputed to have the prettiest lips. The scene is then echoed (or, in Roethlisberger's words, parodied) by the female figures on the right. The artist has chosen to set the scene in an imaginary

106

Italian landscape including the Torre delle Milizie in Rome (the tower in the right background). The strong colour and restless composition is typical of Breenbergh's later years in Amsterdam when references to Italian landscape had to come from his imagination or memory and no longer have the acute sense of place to be found in his early work (p.128). Roethlisberger dates this painting to the mid-1640s by which time artistic fashions in Amsterdam had changed.

Pieter Codde

Amsterdam 1599 – Amsterdam 1678

Pieter Codde's career was spent in Amsterdam although he had contacts with near-by Haarlem which influenced his style. He is said to have been a pupil of Frans Hals and certainly his pictures are very close in style to those of Frans Hals' brother Dirck. The relationship between Frans Hals and Codde was sufficiently close for Codde to complete Hals' *Militia Company* of 1637 (Amsterdam, Rijksmuseum) which Hals had left unfinished. Most of Codde's pictures are militia scenes in interiors and such pictures were especially popular in the 1630s, although they were out of fashion by the middle of the century. Codde also painted a few more emotionally complex pictures such as the justly celebrated *Smoker in a Room* (Lille, Musée des Beaux-Arts) which has been interpreted as an 'allegory of contentment with life'. Codde's style varied little during his long career and his pictures are always highly finished, so in this respect he remained uninfluenced by the freedom of Hals' brushwork.

107. Dutch Cavaliers and their Ladies making Music, 1631
panel; 49.5 × 64.1 cm
Bristol City Art Gallery
The 1631 date is confirmed by the modish high-waisted costume worn by the lady with her back to the spectator. The fashion for elegant companies in interiors was relatively short-lived and soon gave way to a much more intimate depiction of middle-class life which reached its height in the 1660s. This is an especially good example of the well-dressed company enjoying itself, with overtones of misbehaviour. The two figures on the extreme left seem to be amorously engaged and their faces are eagerly expectant.

107 [colour plate VI]

108

Adriaen Tjercksz. Backer

Amsterdam *c.*1635/36 – Amsterdam 1684

This nephew of Jacob Backer achieved some importance in his time for painting the ceiling of the main hall of the Amsterdam town hall (now the Royal Palace). He continued his uncle's tradition of painting subject pictures which are close to the Rembrandtesque tradition. Like other contemporary portrait painters he remained unaffected by Rembrandt's late and free manner, unpopular with the many patrons who preferred a much more meticulous technique and less emotionally charged effect. Backer was also a portrait painter.

108. Croesus and Solon
canvas; 106 × 96.5 cm
Shipley Art Gallery, Gateshead (Tyne and Wear Museums Service)
Until identified recently by Sumowski, this picture bore a

tentative and not unreasonable attribution to Jan Victors who also worked in Rembrandt's manner but not exclusively so. The subject – the concept that wealth does not bring happiness – was a popular one. The pursuit of wealth was, in fact, an overriding concern in the 17th-century Dutch Republic, however much pastors and moralists reacted against it. Croesus, in questioning the philosopher Solon, sees himself as the happiest man in the world because of his great wealth. Solon replies that not until a man is dead can he count himself truly happy. The warning is reinforced in the background of the picture where Croesus' end on a funeral pyre, having lost his wealth and his kingdom, is shown in graphic detail. His last-minute salvation by Apollo is omitted in this essentially Christian moral story.

Jacob Adriaensz. Backer
Harlingen 1608 – Amsterdam 1651

Backer's origins were in Friesland and he was apprenticed in Leeuwarden to Lambert Jacobsz., a painter whose work is rare and hardly represented outside Frisian Museums. Backer became one of Rembrandt's earliest pupils in Amsterdam after the latter's arrival there at the beginning of 1632. From Rembrandt Backer learned a meticulous portrait style which loosened slightly in the 1640s. As a result of Backer's closeness to Rembrandt's portrait style of the 1630s the two artists were often confused in the 18th and 19th centuries. Modern scholarship has had no difficulty in detaching the formal portraits from Rembrandt and giving them to Backer (they often bear his monogram in any case) but the subject pictures have continued to present a problem. At his best, Backer's sober portraits achieve a standard as high as that of any other official portraitist working in Amsterdam in the middle years of the century. He was obviously out of sympathy with the great changes which came over Rembrandt's painting style in the 1640s and this ensured his continued success with the more conservative patrons.

109. A Lady
canvas; 101.6 × 86.3 cm
Trustees of the Holburne Museum, Bath
Even though she is obviously a person of importance, the sitter of this sumptuous portrait has not been identified. It was unusual for the Amsterdam bourgeosie of the time to be quite so ostentatious in the display of jewellery and lace. The costume would indicate a date around 1650 at which period the artist was at the height of his success.

109

110

Gerbrand van den Eeckhout
Amsterdam 1621 – Amsterdam 1674

The whole of Eeckhout's art is indelibly imprinted with that of his master Rembrandt. Unlike so many of Rembrandt's pupils who mastered his style with skill and then developed their own characters, Eeckhout's art remained recognisably Rembrandtesque. His Rembrandtisms were grafted onto his own sense of colour, drawing and composition. Like Rembrandt, Eeckhout painted both portraits and subject pieces, the latter being the more interesting and inventive side of his art; Eeckhout's portraits, in order to be successful with Amsterdam patrons, had to conform to the rather narrow and rigid standards of the day. (On the occasions when Rembrandt rebelled against those standards the result was a dramatic decline in official commissions.) In modern times Eeckhout has not been accorded equal status with such contemporaries in Rembrandt's orbit as Bol and Flinck. This may be because there has been no recent monographic study of his work.

110. Adoration of the Shepherds, 1665
canvas; 49 × 62.2 cm
National Museum of Wales, Cardiff
The superficial debt to Rembrandt in this moving picture is very great. The shadowed treatment of the subject is familiar from Rembrandt's picture of the same subject in the National Gallery, London. However, Eeckhout shows his originality in the sense of drama created by selecting the moment when the shepherds arrive at the stable; they are almost always shown in the act of adoration. The Virgin Mary is still asleep and Joseph looks up in surprise at the shepherds standing at the door. The only source of light is the lantern above the Christ Child's head and the artist has avoided the 'Holy' inner light which appears so often in Rembrandt's work where the figures and indeed whole scenes seem to flow from within. The relative freedom of brushwork must also be derived from Rembrandt.

School of Rembrandt

111. The Angel appearing to Hagar
canvas; 109.5 × 100.5 cm
National Museums and Galleries on Merseyside, Walker Art Gallery, Liverpool
Even though great controversy surrounds the definition of the art of Rembrandt himself, there is even greater, although less acrimonious, disagreement over the definition of the art of his many pupils. This, and the following picture, have been wisely placed by the Walker Art Gallery under the artist's school rather than having unsatisfactory and unconvincing attributions to one or more of the less well-defined pupils. There is, in fact, no specific painting by Rembrandt from which this painting could have been derived although there are drawings by Rembrandt of individual motifs. The dramatic force of this picture lies in the relationship between the angel and the figure of Hagar and this is the essence of what is derived from Rembrandt. The rest of the picture appears eclectic and there are reflections of several different pupils

111 [colour plate XV]

ranging from Jan Lievens, for the treatment of the landscape, to Samuel van Hoogstraten, for the expression on the face of the angel. If a solution is ever found, it is likely to be that this painting is an early work by a Rembrandt pupil who changed his style on maturing. The possible candidates are Ferdinand Bol or Govaert Flinck, but the picture is not close enough to either of them to be attributed without hesitation. The difficulty over attribution has obscured the fact that this is a picture of a very high order and that the traditional attribution to Rembrandt, although wrong on grounds of style, was not far off the mark in terms of quality. There is a perfectly balanced relationship between the two figures.

112. The Betrothal
canvas; 90.8 × 121.7 cm
National Museums and Galleries on Merseyside, Walker Art Gallery, Liverpool
The contrast between this and the other Rembrandt school picture illustrated here (above) could not be greater and on grounds of costume and general style the picture has to date from the decade 1640-50. This means that the picture predates Rembrandt's celebrated *Jewish Bride* by almost twenty years. Here, however, the meaning is not entirely clear. It is not a standard betrothal portrait of actual sitters as the man is in 16th-century costume and the woman in fashionable dress of *c.*1640. It is virtually certain, therefore, that, like the *Jewish Bride*, the picture makes some biblical or historical allusion. The date of this painting makes it a precocious work executed in the full knowledge of Rembrandt's

112

painting style in the 1640s and, as a result, it has been given to almost every one of Rembrandt's pupils in turn.

Rembrandt

Leiden 1606 – Amsterdam 1669

By both popular and scholarly consent, Rembrandt is held to be the greatest of all Dutch painters and one of the great painters of all time. The definition of that greatness is changing as some of the works highest in popular estimation undergo scholarly reappraisal. *The Man in the Golden Helmet* (Berlin-Dahlem, Staatliche Museen), *Saul harping before David* (The Hague, Mauritshuis), *The Polish Rider* (New York, Frick Collection), *The Mill* (Washington, National Gallery) and *The Man in the Armchair* (ex-Chatsworth, now London, National Gallery) are all examples of pictures no longer considered to be by Rembrandt or under serious doubt. Any attempt, therefore, to summarise Rembrandt's achievement has to take into account the overturning of some dearly-held values. A number of pictures now have to be allotted to pupils or placed in a growing and confusing category of 18th-century or even later imitations or pastiches.

Rembrandt was immensely productive in his early years in Leiden when he concentrated on small pictures. The early years in Amsterdam, to which he moved in 1632, included a number of official commissions such as *The Anatomy Lesson of Dr Tulp* (The Hague, Mauritshuis) and numerous portraits. This stage in his career culminated in the unfavourably received *Night Watch* (1641) (Amsterdam, Rijksmuseum). This was followed by a relatively lean period during which he painted few large-scale pictures. A period of intensity returned in the 1650s leading to the

113

114

final decade 1660-69 when a steadily falling output is made up for by an increase in complexity of technique and an approach to the subject which can only be described as universal. In his last pictures Rembrandt tried to define in paint the very essence of the human spirit.

113. Bust of a bearded Man in a Cap
canvas; 78 × 66.7 cm
National Gallery, London
Reproduced by courtesy of the Trustees
The date on this picture has been variously read as 1653 or 1657. The picture falls into a category of Rembrandt's art which is relatively less well-known, heads done as subject pieces rather than as commissioned portraits. Often they are of old men, sometimes Jewish, or they represent Christian saints. This picture seems to be an exercise in pure painting and is not sufficiently highly finished to have been produced for a particular patron. The freedom with which it is executed allows considerable insight into Rembrandt's broad technique. Rembrandt's style was to an extent derived from Venetian 16th-century painters, especially Titian whose art he is known to have admired. Titian, for instance, also set heads against dark and shadowy backgrounds to increase the three-dimensional illusion, an idea that had become quite normal in 17th-century portraiture. Rembrandt took this convention a good deal further as he allowed his shadows to vary in intensity causing a kind of atmospheric smoke to cross the picture surface. In this picture the shadows blur one shoulder and throw the other into much sharper outline. This gives the whole an insubstantial feeling.

Philips Koninck

Amsterdam 1619 – Amsterdam 1688

Koninck perfected a particular type of composition – the vast, broad panorama of the Dutch landscape seen from an imaginary high viewpoint (just possible from a very high church tower such as that of Utrecht Cathedral). Once he had evolved this type of landscape

115

he varied it little, only changing the intensity of the colour slightly as he grew older, introducing stronger blues and greens for the more sombre brown he had used when still under the influence of his master Rembrandt. Koninck also painted a number of rather gloomy figure pieces and portraits in Rembrandt's manner so weak by comparison to the landscapes that it is difficult to imagine that they were painted by the same artist.

114. Extensive Landscape
canvas; 87 × 112.4cm
Southampton City Art Gallery
The picture marks the precise moment when the artist was emerging from the influence of Rembrandt and finding his own way of painting. Up to this moment the landscapes had been rather tentative, small-scale and in brownish tones. They had a Rembrandtesque atmosphere but were not particularly distinguished (see, for example, pictures in the Victoria and Albert Museum, London, and the City Art Gallery, Manchester). Perhaps etchings by Hercules Seghers, which Rembrandt certainly collected, inspired Koninck's panoramic landscapes. The treatment of the infinity of the distance is almost Impressionist in its dissolution of tones and application of thick paint to suggest detail. Even with so much minute incident the artist never loses control of the vastness of the panorama nor allows it to degenerate into mere description. The sands and dunes were usually viewed by other artists from ground level.

Willem van de Velde I

Leiden *c.*1611 – Greenwich 1693

The art of Willem van de Velde the Elder has been overshadowed by the achievements of his illustrious son, Willem van de Velde the Younger, who is usually held to be the best as well as the most famous of all Dutch seascape painters. A high proportion of the father's pictures were executed in a special technique. This consisted of drawing with a reed pen on a white ground and then tinting the whole with a little transparent monochrome to achieve the shadows. This technique demanded a high degree of accuracy and mistakes could not be rectified. It was this elaborate skill which the younger van de Velde derived from his father and which he was able to transform by the use of colour.

115. The Dutch Attack on Harwich, July, 1667, 1669
canvas; 54.5 × 75cm
National Maritime Museum
This picture depicts one of the two attacks made by the Dutch on the English in 1667 (see p.146 for *The Dutch burning the English Fleet at Chatham* by Schellincks). Van de Velde has used the incident as an excuse for an elaborate piece of ship portraiture rather than for a dramatic military composition as was preferred by Schellincks. For sheer accuracy of drawing, van de Velde was unequalled and such ships might be reconstructed from the information he provides.

Simon de Vlieger

Rotterdam *c.*1600 ? – Weesp 1653

De Vlieger occupies a pivotal place in the history of Dutch seascape painting between the early developments of Porcellis and the masterpieces of Jan van de Cappelle and Willem van de Velde the Younger. This can be seen in the gradual evolution of his art. His work in the 1630s tended to be monochrome in the Porcellis tradition, but gradually became more monumental in scale and displayed a greater interest in colour. By the end of his career in the late 1640s, de Vlieger was influenced by the early work of Jan van de Cappelle introducing more static compositions with a greater emphasis on atmosphere and compositional order than on the exact detail of the ships.

116. A Dutch Ferry Boat before a Breeze
canvas; 84 × 85.1 cm
National Maritime Museum
De Vlieger's range was wide as he could describe storms and absolute calm with equal ability. In this picture the description of a choppy sea is perfect and the main boat daringly placed in the centre of the composition. Even if de Vlieger's pictures lack the monumentality of the great pictures of Jan van de Cappelle and Willem van de Velde II, few seascape painters had a greater understanding of the feel of the sea and

116

rendered it with greater naturalism. Compare, for instance, van Goyen's treatment of water (p.60) where it appears much more schematised.

Jan van de Cappelle

Amsterdam *c.*1626 – Amsterdam 1679

Relatively little is known about Jan van de Cappelle but he seems to have been one of the most interesting figures of his time in Amsterdam, both as a collector and as a painter. He was financially secure as his family owned a dye works and it has even been thought that his paintings were 'amateur', in the best sense of the word, which would explain their comparative rarity. He painted both seascapes and winter landscapes. The seascapes are unified by a sense of restraint. All detail is subordinated to the tonality of the whole and the ships are massed against the sky in unrealistic groupings as the overriding intention was compositional balance. Van de Cappelle's early works owe a debt to Simon de Vlieger, but this influence soon disappears and the artist made no reference to contemporary developments in seascape paintings in Amsterdam by Bakhuyzen and Willem van de Velde the Younger. The calm mood of his pictures did have some influence on other painters, especially Hendrick Dubbels whose seascapes have sometimes been confused with his own. De Cappelle's winter scenes are rare and they too make no reference to other local painters of winter landscapes such as Aert van der Neer.

117 [colour plate X]

117. Winter Scene
canvas; 45 × 56 cm
Private Collection, on loan to the Birmingham City Museums and Art Gallery
This is a very fine example of a winter scene by van de Cappelle. Distinctive is the way in which the artist imposes an austere geometry on each element just as Saenredam did in his church interiors. The result is self-conscious, with the trees and houses huddled unnaturally close together, but the whole picture remains convincing as a depiction of a frozen waterway in a Dutch village. The figures are typical of the artist's rather generalised approach to them even though they strike up realistic poses, as in the group huddled over the hole in the ice anticipating a catch. Few other landscapes of the 17th century achieved such formal order with such economy of means. This picture was first recorded in a sale in Amsterdam in 1775 and was in the collection of Sir Alfred Beit, London, by 1900 (Russell, nos. 151 and 176).

Bartholomeus van der Helst
Amsterdam 1613 – Amsterdam 1670

In terms of his reputation and achievement Bartholomeus van der Helst was the most important portraitist in 17th-century Amsterdam. He executed a series of truly spectacular large-scale group portraits (Amsterdam, Rijksmuseum) in a robust realistic style which had a far greater contemporary appeal than did the brooding and introspective work of Rembrandt. In common with a number of Dutch painters of the time (especially in Haarlem as well as Amsterdam) van der Helst evolved his own special brand of realism. This can be defined as a remarkable truth to nature – he does not, for instance, generally flatter his sitters – but he combines this with an overall sense of decorative effect and colour balance. This down-to-earth approach is quite the opposite of the late work of Frans Hals who made no concessions to the sensuality of surface texture.

118 [colour plate XIII]

118. Portrait of a Dutch Rear-Admiral, 1662
canvas; 113 × 91.4 cm

119

Glasgow Art Gallery and Museum
Even though, for van der Helst, the picture is on a relatively small scale it epitomises his style. The eye is drawn across all the brilliantly rendered surfaces, of cloth, embroidery, metal, lace, etc., but the artist keeps all these surfaces under control through a careful gradation of tone towards the edges of the canvas. This system of avoiding sharp contrasts near the edges of the canvas was exploited to the full by Rembrandt whose sitters emerge from the gloom. Although the sitter in this picture has not been identified, he is likely to have been a naval commander of some importance owing to the sumptuous way in which he is dressed. The date of 1662 on the picture is useful for the costume historian because the number of dated Dutch pictures in this period is surprisingly small.

Gerbrand van den Eeckhout
(for bibliography see p.130)

119. Four Officers of the Amsterdam Wine Coopers' and Wine Rackers' Guild, 1657
canvas; 163 × 197.1 cm
National Gallery, London
Reproduced by courtesy of the Trustees
This picture is the only large-scale example of a Dutch group portrait in a British public collection. Most group portraits, apart from the celebrated series by Frans Hals in Haarlem and Rembrandt's *Night Watch*, remain in the smaller town museums of the Netherlands where they form a valuable link with the local past.

The formal nature of this portrait is emphasised by the inscription of the sitters' names on the document on the table. Furthermore, the artist has abandoned his Rembrandtesque style in favour of the realist tradition which dominates the group portraits of Bartholomeus van der Helst. The composition is a skilful arrangement of four men, dressed almost identically in black, round a table. The barely visible painting in the background represents the patron saint of the Coopers' Guild.

Willem Kalf

Rotterdam 1619 – Amsterdam 1693

Kalf was one of the most talented of all Dutch still-life painters. He lacked the passion for overall detail and clarity which characterises Haarlem still-life painters such as Pieter Claesz. and the two Hedas. Instead he partly conceals the main elements in shadow and understates every object. Minute pinpoints of light pick out the weave of carpets and only the highlights of his glasses are seen. In spite of the fact that most of the elements in his pictures are simple enough, especially compared with the sumptuousness of an Abraham van Beyeren, his pictures have a sense of opulence which no other Dutch still-life painter achieves. He painted relatively few pictures.

120

120. Still-Life with Fruit, a Goblet and a Salver
canvas; 58.9 × 50.7 cm
Manchester City Art Galleries
Placing the still-life elements on a ledge was a common device for it allowed the artist to display them with clarity, here only a rummer, a wine goblet, fruit, a salver and a carpet, characteristic of Kalf's austere style. Kalf's sense of design and restraint with colour lies behind his reputation in this century. He avoided anecdote, rarely included elements which could be described as Vanitas and he seems to have delighted in the objects for their own sake.

Abraham van Beyeren

The Hague 1620/21 – Overschie 1690

Van Beyeren is now known as the most important and prolific of Dutch banquet scene painters, but he was a versatile artist who could produce convincing sea pieces in the tradition of Porcellis and van Goyen as well as still-lifes of dead fish.

His banquet pieces unite all the disparate elements of still-life painting developing in the first half of the century. The Haarlem painters, especially Pieter Claesz. and the two Hedas, had concentrated on a certain austerity both of composition and colour. The opposite had been practised by Jan Davidsz. de Heem first in Utrecht and later in Antwerp. Van Beyeren's elaborate and almost Baroque effects owe a good deal to the de

121 [colour plate XIV]

122

Heem tradition but remain somewhat austere in the treatment of individual objects. He used a wide variety of objects, fruit, meat, game, silver and often a brilliant red, cooked lobster.

121. Still-Life with Lobster, Fruit and China Ware
canvas; 98.4 × 84.5 cm
Dundee Museums and Art Galleries
In terms of balance, colour and sumptuousness of effect on a relatively limited scale, this is one of van Beyeren's most satisfactory compositions. Such pictures were known by the Dutch as 'banketjes' (literally banquet pieces). They obviously satisfied the bourgeois longing for extravagance symbolising wealth and status. The objects depicted in this picture were indeed luxurious in their time because oranges and lemons had to be brought laboriously and unsafely by sea from the Mediterranean round the Bay of Biscay, running the gauntlet of the enemy Spanish (until 1648) and of pirates. Elaborate silver objects were immensely expensive as were such textiles as velvet, generally imported from France or Italy. Van Beyeren very rarely included a Vanitas element into his depiction of riches. He does include his own reflection mirrored in the silver ewer, an idea repeated in some other compositions (*eg* Cleveland, Ohio, Museum of Art in which the ewer appears as here).

Pieter Janssens Elinga
working Rotterdam *c.*1650 – Amsterdam ? after 1682

Almost nothing is known of the career of this talented artist. His reputation has been overshadowed by that of Pieter de Hooch and Elinga's carefully considered and beautifully lit bourgeois domestic interiors owe a considerable debt to those of de Hooch. Indeed, until recently, many of his pictures were wrongly attributed to de Hooch. Elinga was also a still-life painter of much greater originality.

122. Still-Life with Bread, Lemons, a Jug and a Glass
canvas; 80.8 × 65.4 cm
Ferens Art Gallery : Hull City Museums and Art Galleries
This still-life conforms to the type most commonly found in Dutch painting – of everyday but inexpensive objects simply arranged. The jug is likely to be Delftware and the glass a standard pattern used at the time. It is unlikely that the picture has any moral overtones as there are no flowers (almost all of which could have symbolic meaning) and no Vanitas elements. The careful way in which the composition is built up is reminiscent of Willem Kalf who often left a large part of the background in deep shadow. Like Kalf, but unlike most other still-life painters of the time, Elinga uses a certain softness in the treatment of the individual elements.

Aert van der Neer
Gorinchem 1603/04 – Amsterdam 1677

In common with a number of landscape painters (especially Hobbema), Aert van der Neer began painting in a rather clumsy manner without any of the refinement characteristic of his long if uneventful career. His work divides conveniently into two categories – the moonlight scenes, mostly on rivers, and the winter scenes. His early work included rather claustrophobic woodland and forest scenes which are individual in their approach and not derivative from Cornelis Vroom.

Aert van der Neer was prolific and varied his repertoire and scale but little. His pictures are usually of medium size with only a few compositional motifs skilfully varied for each picture. His especial talent was the treatment of light. He was equally good at the still effect of moonlight and the cold but sometimes almost pink light of a frosty day. His occasional experiments with light and composition (opposite) placed him on a level with his greater landscape contemporaries.

123

124

125

123. 'Twilight'
panel; 32.3 × 25.4cm
National Loan Collection Trust, Cannon Hall Museum, Barnsley Metropolitan Borough Council
This picture still bears its 'Romantic' title probably provided in the 18th or early-19th century. It shows an inn on the edge of a village at evening. Such subtle effects are rare in the art of van der Neer and this yellowish light, rare in Holland in nature, is more characteristic of the Italianate landscapists such as Jan Both (p.50) and Cornelis van Poelenburgh (p.49). The composition too is unusually broad in effect due to the low viewpoint. It is as if the painter was sitting on the ground in order to give the trees a dominating scale.

124. Moonlit Landscape on a River
canvas; 82.7 × 98.2cm
Norfolk Museums Service (Norwich Castle Museum)
A very high proportion of Aert van der Neer's pictures are variations on the theme of the moonlit landscape. This example probably dates from his early years when he executed a number of rather original woodland scenes, a type of picture he later abandoned, and this ambitiously-scaled painting may mark a transition in his work. Typically the composition is rather artificial and the combination of building, trees and water does not record the contemporary Dutch small town or village. As always with van der Neer, the night effect, the figures and the animals are all beautifully considered.

125. A Town on a Frozen River
canvas; 43.8 × 51.4cm
The National Trust, Polesden Lacey (Greville Collection)
Aert van der Neer's townscapes were always fanciful in their treatment of the architecture and included more open space than there was in contemporary Dutch towns. This is an exceptionally fine example of van der Neer's essentially repetitive art.

126. Skating on a Frozen River
canvas; 37.3 × 48.4cm
Royal Pavilion, Art Gallery and Museums, Brighton

126

Despite the repetitious nature of Aert van der Neer's winter scenes, the understanding of atmosphere raises the picture above the average. The treatment of the bare trees and their arrangement is reminiscent of Jan van de Cappelle (p.137) and the apparently casual arrangement of the figures on the ice is masterly. Yet the contrast with van de Cappelle could not be greater as van der Neer is interested in the anecdotal and picturesque. The figures engage in activities and conversations and lack the intensity of those of van de Cappelle. The small scale of this picture has allowed the artist much greater subtlety than is usual with his larger winter scenes such as the particularly ambitious one at Leicester. The quality of this picture is more evident as a result of recent cleaning.

Meindert Hobbema

Amsterdam 1638 – Amsterdam 1709

Until very recently Hobbema was considered to be the greatest of all Dutch landscape painters, even being placed above Jacob van Ruisdael both in popular and informed estimation. Now the position is reversed as Hobbema is seen as a painter whose vision was derivative from his master Jacob van Ruisdael and his independence of spirit, even when it showed itself, is now considered too pretty and lacking in bite. Even Hobbema's *The Avenue* (London, National Gallery) has slipped from the universal esteem in which it was held for more than a century. This reassessment of Hobbema's relative position should not lead to his achievements being underestimated. He was the true inventor of the picturesque wooded landscape and as such was the ancestor of two centuries of landscape painting, especially in England and in 19th-century Holland (the Koekkoek family). His career falls into three distinct phases with a large group of rapidly executed but rather hesitant early works, a small number of Ruisdael-inspired woodland scenes and about a hundred grand picturesque landscapes which culminate, unexpectedly, in *The Avenue*.

127

127. A Waterfall in a Wood
panel; 26.7 × 22.3 cm
Trustees of the National Galleries of Scotland, Edinburgh
This is one of Hobbema's most perfectly realised small-scale pictures in the manner of Jacob van Ruisdael. Ruisdael must have imposed a severe discipline on Hobbema as the pictures, which can be dated before their association in Haarlem *c.*1660, are much more freely painted and lack the determination of the later works. All the compositional elements found in Ruisdael are present, from the running water to the fallen tree trunk. There can, however, be no such allegorical significance in such a composition as can be argued for Ruisdael and the elements are purely picturesque. Indeed, close inspection of the background of this picture reveals little twists and turns of the brush which are intended to charm the spectator into a visual exploration of the picturesque undergrowth.

128

128. Landscape with a Coppice
canvas; 89 × 113 cm
The National Trust, Petworth House (Egremont Collection)
Most of Hobbema's large landscapes of this type are in British collections with the result that they have become almost too familiar. The debt to Ruisdael here is not as great as in the earlier work (opposite) and the artist has concentrated on the picturesque aspects of the woodland scene. It has often been suggested that these pictures are based on a type of woodland common in the Dutch Province of Gelderland but the number of Hobbema's compositional elements is so limited that it is unlikely that such pictures were based on an actual site. The artist has used his favourite device of a vignette on the left through which the eye is allowed to travel into the far distance. The lightness of such passages anticipates the art of Constable.

Jacob van Ruisdael

(for biography see p.92)

129. A Waterfall
canvas; 101.3 × 82 cm
National Trust, Petworth House (Egremont Collection)
Compared to the *River in Spate* at Bristol (p.94), this is a much more dense and moody picture incorporating all Ruisdael's most serious and melancholy elements. The blackish sky echoes the mood of the broken tree on the lower left. The dramatic waterfall occupies almost the whole of the lower part of the picture. Such pictures have been interpreted as the endless cycle of nature and the precariously perched castle ruin in the background as a symbol of the frailty of man before the power of nature.

129

130. Winter Landscape
canvas; 43.8 × 52.8 cm
Private Collection, on loan to Birmingham City Museums and Art Gallery
From the 1660s onwards in Amsterdam, Jacob van Ruisdael painted a small number of small-scale winter landscapes which are considered to be among his best works. His treatment of the frost and cold is the exact opposite of the picturesque charm of Aert van der Neer (p.140f), although in sensitivity he approaches the perfection of Jan van de Cappelle (p.117f). Even though at first sight landscapes such as these seem accurately observed, they rarely depict an actual site. Instead Ruisdael chose to alter the natural phenomena into an elaborately thought-out composition which seems so natural because it is so carefully contrived.

The painting is recorded in the collection by Hofstede de Groot, nos.998 and 1030, and Rosenberg, no.617.

130 [colour plate XXI]

131

Adriaen van de Velde

Amsterdam 1636 – Amsterdam 1672

Adriaen van de Velde was the son of Willem van de Velde the Elder and the brother of Willem van de Velde the Younger. His style was unrelated to theirs and depended much more on that of Berchem and Potter. In other words, most of van de Velde's work balances uneasily between the Italianate and the realistic in landscape. However, he had great skill with figures and animals and he was much in demand as a collaborator (see Jan van der Heyden, p.150f), for example with Jan Wijnants and, occasionally, with Hobbema. Velde's pictures are characterised by a strident blue in the sky, well-painted animals and a relaxed quality of composition. In general he was repetitious but he did paint a few totally idiosyncratic pictures. The best of these is *The Farm* (Berlin - Dahlem, Staatliche Museen) which is a pure landscape, very densely wooded but with shafts of light breaking up the trees and this anticipates landscape painting in the 19th century.

131. Landscape – a Woman milking a Cow, 1669
canvas; 31.1 × 38.7cm
National Loan Collection Trust, Cannon Hall Museum, Barnsley Metropolitan Borough Council
This picture was described by John Smith as 'a beautiful production' in 1834 at the time when the fashion was for artificial rather than naturalistic landscape paintings. The artist has made his customary compromise between Mediterranean light and Northern subject. The humdrum activity of milking is made artificially 'pastoral', the herdsman, with his back to the spectator, surveys an unnaturally elegant scene while the milkmaid ignores her task to gaze at her male admirer. There are no stylistic reasons for not accepting Smith's date, which he read as 1669, as the artist did not make any great changes to his style during his relatively short career.

Willem Schellincks

Amsterdam 1627 ? – Amsterdam 1678

Schellincks characteristically painted Italianate landscapes and he was influenced by Jan Asselijn especially. Confusion between the two artists has been clarified by Steland-Stief's book on Asselijn. Schellincks painted a wide variety of other subjects ranging from harbour scenes to winter landscapes. He visited England at some undocumented moment in his career, a visit principally recorded by numerous topographical drawings.

132

133

132. The Dutch burning the English Fleet at Chatham, 1665
panel; 23.5 × 33 cm
Maidstone Museum, Kent Archaeological Society Collections
This picture records one of the less glorious episodes in the reign of Charles II, regarded at the time as a major disaster. Paintings of the England of Charles II are rare so that this is a precious survival even though it is not a work of very high quality. The castle and cathedral of Rochester are placed somewhat fancifully on the right with the burning ships at Chatham beyond.

Jan Victors

Amsterdam 1619/20 – Dutch East India 1676 or earlier

Jan Victors might be described as the most wayward of Rembrandt's pupils as he ended up so far from his master's style that it is impossible to tell that Rembrandt had had any involvement in his development. In common with almost all Rembrandt's pupils, Victors assimilated his master's style without losing his independence. His paintings are usually large-scale biblical pieces with many figures painted in a light-toned palette. He also painted severe Rembrandtesque portraits. Towards the end of his career it must have become increasingly obvious that the strictly-controlled 'Rembrandt manner' was less and less in demand and in response to this Victors changed his style drastically. He became a painter of banal but endearing genre subjects such as cows being ferried across water in small boats.

133. Landscape with a Cow in a Ferry Boat
canvas; 83 × 115.3 cm
National Museums and Galleries on Merseyside, Walker Art Gallery, Liverpool
This is a late genre work by Jan Victors when he had abandoned all trace of the influence of Rembrandt. The treatment of the subject seems rather old-fashioned and almost naïve. There is none of the clear, cold treatment of landscape which became so popular in Amsterdam in the 1660s and 1670s but instead a dense texture of greys and browns. The artist had learnt from Rembrandt to relate his figures through facial expressions; the cow's gaze as it is ferried somewhat unsteadily across the narrow stretch of water is worth observing. The picture illustrates the complete orderliness of the Dutch countryside at this date, a dramatic contrast to much of Midland and Northern England which remained unenclosed until the 18th century.

Willem van de Velde II

Leiden *c.*1633 – Greenwich 1707

He was a pupil of his father Willem van de Velde the Elder, the specialist in monochrome sea pieces. Willem van de Velde the Younger is perhaps the best-known of all Dutch seascape painters and was undoubtedly one of the best as well as one of the most prolific. Of all his Dutch contemporaries he employed the greatest number of studio assistants, no doubt because of the technical difficulty of turning out numerous complex sea pieces on demand. The first half of his career was spent in Amsterdam where his style formed and matured. There were many influences upon it in these early years and these reappeared during his later career in England.

Van de Velde had two distinct manners of painting which were opposed to one another in mood and style. His stormy sea pieces are the less personal and were

134 [colour plate XXII]

derived from Ludolf Bakhuyzen who became Amsterdam's leading seascape painter after the departure of van de Velde. His calm manner was more distinctive as it ran parallel with the achievement of Jan van de Cappelle without imitating it. Van de Velde's calms have a delicacy and poetry in the treatment of light which transcends their primary purpose as ship portraits. After van de Velde came to England and was granted a studio at Greenwich (in the 1670s) his art became less precise and more 'extrovert' and in this manner he depicted the numerous naval battles between the English and the Dutch. The studio played a critical part as the scale of his pictures increased. The influence of the van de Veldes on English 18th- and early 19th-century seascape painting cannot be overestimated and it proved difficult for English painters such as Monamy and Brooking to break away from the tradition established by the van de Veldes.

134. The English Ship, the 'Hampton Court' in a Storm
canvas; 105.4 × 119.4 cm
Birmingham City Museums and Art Gallery
Most of van de Velde's English ships are studio works rather than autograph. In this instance the quality and refinement of the painting suggests that the artist alone was responsible. The treatment of the background storm is derived from Bakhuizen although the dramatic and original composition is very much van de Velde's own. Such ship portraits do not appear in England before van de Velde as no English artist seems to have been capable of the complex skills required to achieve such a *tour de force* of perspective, detail and nautical

accuracy. The *Hampton Court* was launched in 1678 and the painting probably dates from shortly after.

Otto Marseus van Schrieck
Nijmegen *c.*1619/20 – Amsterdam 1678

The importance of Marseus van Schrieck has been underestimated as he was the originator and perfector of a particular genre – the forest floor. This genre delights in slugs, snails, lizards, frogs, snakes and other forms of insect and reptile life. These creatures are always painted with deceptive realism as individual studies but are placed in an artificially densely-populated environment for decorative effect. The result can be sinister as so many of these creatures are symbols of death and decay and it is hard to avoid the conclusion that this meaning was intended. His pictures, however, generally lack specific *memento mori*, unlike those of Matthias Withoos. Marseus van Schrieck exerted a profound influence on Lachtropius, Rachel Ruysch and Matthias Withoos.

135. Silver Birch Trunk with Animals and Insects
canvas; 61.7 × 52.3 cm
The Syndics of the Fitzwilliam Museum, Cambridge
Until recently this picture was attributed to Rachel Ruysch although it is rather different in style and handling to her work (p.152). This painting is altogether more sensual and more sinister. The perfection of the dog-rose is contrasted with the overturned toadstool (a symbol of decay) and the frightening movement of the snake which is making a strike in the direction of the lizard. There are other emotive symbols such as the snail crawling up the tree trunk. The butterflies are introduced as symbols of transience rather than as diverting decoration as they appear in the Rachel Ruysch.

135

Nicolaes Lachtropius
working Amsterdam ?*c.*1666 – *c.*1700

Little is known about the career of Lachtropius who was both a flower painter and a 'forest floor' specialist (see under Marseus van Schrieck, above, for a discussion of this genre). In general style his flower pieces conform to the taste of the later part of the century for greater clarity in contrast to the overblown Baroque of Mignon and de Heem.

136. A Vase of Flowers
canvas; 56 × 48.8 cm
The Syndics of the Fitzwilliam Museum, Cambridge
The simplicity of this composition indicates a relatively late date when Lachtropius, like Simon Verelst (p.69), reduced

136 [colour plate XXIII]

137

138

the number of flowers in a composition. The principal flowers, hollyhock, mallow, convolvulus, sunflower, thistle and zinnia, all bloom in August. The domination of the hollyhock is especially bold and unusual as the predominance of one flower is generally avoided.

Jacob van Walscapelle

Dordrecht 1644 – Amsterdam 1727

Walscapelle's paintings are very rare and he may have pursued another occupation, which was quite common in such centres as Amsterdam where the competition among artists was fierce. Walscapelle made no original contribution to the development of flower painting but continued the Baroque tradition established by Jan Davidsz. de Heem with complete meticulousness.

137. A Vase of Flowers
canvas; 57.4 × 44.2 cm
The Syndics of the Fitzwilliam Museum, Cambridge
This is a typical example of Walscapelle's elaborate style which subordinates the natural characteristics of the flowers to a complex and decorative arrangement of stems, leaves and ears of wheat. The main flowers are poppies, peonies, tulips, marigolds, convolvulus and snowball flowers. The flowers are not united by a season (unlike most of the other flower pieces in this exhibition (pp.68, 74, 101, 111, 148, 149) because the painter is interested in a decorative rather than naturalistic effect. The flowers are less confidently treated than by Lachtropius (p.148) as each one is played down to complete the decorative ideal.

Jan van der Heyden

Gorinchem 1637 – Amsterdam 1712

Van der Heyden has always been recognised as the most meticulous and refined of all the Dutch townscape painters. His art is in fact more complex and his stylistic development more interesting than has hitherto been thought. He started by painting farmyard scenes which lack the clarity and dignity to be found in his mature work. These pictures are often signed even

139

though in recent years they have been obstinately attributed to other painters. They reveal their author, however, in the meticulous, and indeed almost obsessive way each individual brick and stone is painted. Van der Heyden soon abandoned these homespun scenes and turned to two specific kinds of architectural painting. The first and more popular today represented Amsterdam and its neighbours (Delft, Emmerich and as far afield as Brussels and Cologne). The second and more inventive variety combined real buildings with architectural inventions convincing enough to have been built. In his last years van der Heyden's style changed quite radically, no doubt in response to changes in fashion at the turn of the century. He painted a small group of landscapes whose great detail creates an almost surreal atmosphere. The same might be said of his very rare still-life paintings in which precious objects are piled one upon another with an unreal and disquieting effect. Like other Dutch painters, van der Heyden had other interests, in his case fire-fighting and fire-prevention in Amsterdam.

138. A Village Scene with a Woman at a Well
panel; 56.7 × 72.2 cm
Cooper Art Gallery Trustees, Barnsley Metropolitan Borough Council
In recent years this picture has been attributed to Emanuel Meurant despite a van der Heyden signature. This is because van der Heyden's early work has been little studied and specialists have been reluctant to accept that an artist of such refinement could have begun with such modest subject-matter. In fact this picture bears all the marks of an artist of ability and the humdrum scene is painted with great precision and detachment. Van der Heyden never introduced anecdote into his pictures and the figure here is observed as if she were some object of still-life rather than as a human being animating the scene.

139. A View along a Canal
panel; 38 × 53.3 cm
National Loan Collection Trust, Cannon Hall Museum, Barnsley Metropolitan Borough Council
In the early 19th century this picture was described as a view along the Singel Canal in Amsterdam, but it is likely that this

140 [colour plate XXVII]

is an invented scene made up from buildings in different parts of Amsterdam. The view is more open and picturesque than the newly-laid out Amsterdam canals were in reality. This picture is typical of van der Heyden's concern in mid-career for architectural detail. Also characteristic is the care for tonal unity. The figures in this picture have always been attributed to Adriaen van de Velde who collaborated with a number of landscape painters including van der Heyden.

140. Figures resting and promenading in an Oak Forest
canvas; 28.8 × 33.6cm
Bristol City Art Gallery
Van der Heyden turned to landscape at the end of his long career at a time when the mainstream of Dutch landscape painting had returned to an Italianate or French classically influenced style. Van der Heyden did not build on the great tradition brought to its conclusion by the mature masterpieces of Jacob van Ruisdael but started by looking at the local landscape afresh. As a specialist in townscape, and the most meticulous perfectionist of all in that genre, he treated the woodland in this picture as if it were a static street scene. The artist lavished the same amount of detail on his trees as he did on the brickwork of his houses and churches. The result is almost hallucinatory. The artist's inability to render atmospheric distance means that all the elements seem to be at almost the same distance from the spectator. This technique was used very much more deliberately by the Surrealists early in the 20th century. Such pictures as this one had neither precedent nor succession in Dutch 17th-century painting and their very originality has denied them importance in the general context of painting of the period.

Rachel Ruysch
Amsterdam 1664 – Amsterdam 1750

Rachel Ruysch was arguably the most important painter of flowers of her generation. Her career included the last quarter of the 17th century and the first half of the 18th. She has been included here because a number of her most important works were executed before 1700 and her style modified but little thereafter. Like many contemporary flower painters she also painted 'forest floor' pieces (for which see Marseus van Schrieck, p.148). Ruysch's special contribution to the art of flower painting was one of extreme skill. She was quite simply better than most at describing the texture of petals and she was more inventive than most in composition. Her use of colour was also very personal as she adopted a palette dominated by red, blue and white from the end of the century onwards.

141. Stream in a Dell with Flowers and Reptiles
canvas; 49.8 × 66.6cm
The Syndics of the Fitzwilliam Museum, Cambridge
Although Rachel Ruysch is justly famed for her flower pieces, some of her early works are different in type and mood. The date of this picture must be relatively early in the artist's career, probably in the 1690s, by comparison with other similar but dated works. The 'forest floor' specialists created pictures which were rather sinister in mood – a number of them have an allegorical or Vanitas meaning. Here the artist delights in the painting of small creatures such as the lizard as it devours a butterfly. The treatment of the plants, especially the poppy, is self-consciously Baroque and they are twisted into artificial decorative patterns rather than arranged in a naturalistic way as, for example, in the paintings of Lachtropius (p.148).

Gérard de Lairesse
Liège 1640 – Amsterdam 1711

Like many painters working in the Dutch Republic in the last years of the 17th century, de Lairesse was essentially an eclectic artist. This makes his style impossible to pinpoint to a particular place (he worked in The Hague and Amsterdam). The origins of his art in Liège are clear enough but soon gave way to French and Italian influences, especially from French artists such as Charles Le Brun, who were themselves deeply influenced by Italy. In mid-career de Lairesse went blind and he devoted his last years to the writing of a theoretical treatise on painting, *Groot Schilderboek*, which is one of the few such works written in the Dutch Republic throughout the whole 17th century.

141

142

142. The Meeting of Jacob and Rachel at the Well
canvas; 113 × 192 cm
Kilmarnock and Loudoun District Museums, Dick Institute, Kilmarnock
The frieze-like composition of the figures in this picture and the landscape background both owe a direct debt to French classical painting of the middle years of the 17th century. In this de Lairesse was following the fashion of the 1660s when erudite and elegant overtones were added to homespun Dutch themes. In subject painting truth to nature was abandoned and de Lairesse sets this Old Testament subject in the Roman Campagna. The ambitious scale of this picture is much closer to French pictures than to the generally more modest Dutch pictures of the period.

Arnold Houbraken

Dordrecht 1660 – Amsterdam 1719

Houbraken today is remembered for a three-volume book, *De Groote Schouburgh der Nederlantsche Konstschilders en Schilderessen* (published posthumously in 1726) which contained biographies of the majority of 17th-century painters in the Netherlands. Modern archival research generally supports Houbraken's information even if specific details are sometimes garbled. Houbraken's views were remarkably balanced given the wild prejudices of his own time. He failed to mention either Vermeer of Delft or Hobbema but the work of both these artists had fallen into total neglect by 1700. An example of Houbraken's painting is included here as a token of the state into which Dutch painting had declined by the early years of the 18th century with a few notable exceptions such as van der Werff (whom Houbraken regarded as one of the greatest of all Dutch painters!).

143. Susanna and the Elders
canvas; 36.5 × 27.3 cm
Manchester City Art Galleries
Even though Houbraken had trained under Samuel van Hoogstraten in the northern city of Dordrecht, his art succumbed very quickly to the French classicising taste which swept through Dutch art in the last quarter of the century. Houbraken was not particularly good at imitating this fashionable ideal; there is an uneasy relationship between his figures and their poses are derivative.

143

Public Collections of Dutch 17th-century Paintings in Great Britain

A history of public collecting in the British Isles cannot be attempted until the holdings of each collection have been accurately listed and published. Fortunately, Dutch 17th-century painting is better documented than that of most other schools though there are many gaps in the histories of pictures in the smaller collections.

With a very few exceptions, Dutch pictures in British public collections reflect the specific interests or tastes of a number of individual benefactors. Because the process of collecting and benefaction has been going on for some two hundred years, the history of *private collecting* is reflected in these now static collections. These range from the miscellaneous collection of Dr William Hunter given to Glasgow University in the 1780s to the very recently-formed and specialised collection of Dutch pictures bequeathed by Harold Samuel to the Mansion House in the City of London in 1988.

Royal and aristocratic collectors generally purchased expensively and prestigiously, rarely setting new fashions and more often following those established. One example of such collecting, by the Prince Regent, survives intact in the Royal Collection and demonstrates very clearly his preference for genre painting and in particular for works of the Leiden school. His taste was shared by his friend the 3rd Marquess of Hertford. The character of Hertford's collection was modified by the even more extensive purchasing of his successor, the 4th Marquess, and the efforts of both are represented by the Wallace Collection given to the public in 1899 which exemplifies aristocratic collecting over two generations. The dominating features are genre, especially from Leiden and Amsterdam, and landscape, especially from Amsterdam. Rembrandt and his school are heavily represented. Conspicuous by their absence are Haarlem landscapists such as Jan van Goyen and Salomon van Ruysdael. Still-life is hardly represented at all and all the flower pieces are from the 18th century.

No other aristocratic collection of importance has entered the public domain as a direct bequest, Petworth being the sole example of this type of collection in the custody of the National Trust, but there are a number of significant collections which represent foreign taste in Dutch pictures. The most important of these is that at Dulwich. The history of the Dulwich Collection is well enough known and it is clear that a good number of the Dutch pictures were on the French art market in the later 18th century before they became part of the Sir Peter Francis Bourgeois Bequest to Dulwich in 1811. These pictures, the first major Dutch works to be on public view in England (Dr Hunter's Rembrandt and Koninck were, of course, already in Glasgow University), were extremely influential on public taste. They reflect conventional 18th-century attitudes such as the preference in landscape for the Italianates such as Aelbert Cuyp and Jan Both. There is a large collection of works by Wouwermans. Some odd examples of unexpected artists (mostly relatively minor) show a broader taste than that of the Prince Regent.

The young Ruskin, who lived near Dulwich, developed a resolute hatred of Dutch pictures based on his experience of that collection. Indeed, with the exception of a perfect small work by Jacob van Ruisdael, there are no naturalistic landscapes at Dulwich – even the Hobbema is very heavily worked and artificially composed. This meant that by the 1840s the Dulwich Collection stood for all that was retrogressive in the Old Masters as far as contemporary critical taste was concerned.

Constable's famous comment deprecating Berchem and his influence was also symptomatic of the times. Constable had opposed the founding of the National Gallery and the early years of that institution witness to the relatively narrow range of Dutch painting that was then approved. Works by Rembrandt were acquired early on (including significant ones) but it is not until the mid-19th century that the National Gallery began to build up a significant collection of Dutch pictures beginning with the landscapes in the Wynn Ellis Bequest.

Two other 'foreign' public collections (the Bowes Collection, Barnard Castle, and the de Ferrieres Collection, Cheltenham) were created towards the end of the 19th century, by which time the pre-eminence of the National Gallery Collection had been established. Earlier in the century this position seemed unlikely since two other major institutions (Cambridge and Glasgow) had received gifts and bequests of very great significance. Viscount Fitzwilliam's founding bequest to the University of Cambridge in 1816 brought together a number of very distinguished Dutch pictures, especially genre pieces. This collection was further enriched with the Daniel Mesman Bequest in 1834 although the gift mostly contained pictures by artists then considered to be minor. Recent cleaning and re-examination of these Mesman pictures has resulted in a much higher estimation of their status and thanks to the much later addition of the Broughton Collection of flower pieces, the Fitzwilliam Museum remains by far the largest and most significant collection of Dutch pictures outside London.

The McLellan Collection which came to Glasgow in the 1850s contained over four hundred Old Master pictures, many of them Dutch. This gave the city of Glasgow the largest municipal collection of Dutch pictures in the country. All the McLellan pictures were uneven in quality and this goes for the Dutch too, but the relatively catholic Victorian taste that this represents had the merit of including little-known or minor works which contribute to the wider panorama of creative activity in 17th-century Holland. There is no evidence, however, that Victorian collectors achieved this consciously. The great exception to this generalisation was William Roscoe of Liverpool who formed a great collection of early Italian pictures with regard to their historical significance (many of which are now in the Walker Art Gallery, Liverpool) but Roscoe never turned his attention to Dutch pictures.

The year 1870 marks a turning point in the history of the public collecting of Dutch pictures and until about that time standards were consistently high and copies and inferior works relatively few. Modern scholarship has cast few doubts on the Dutch paintings in the Torrie Collection bequeathed to the University of Edinburgh in 1835. But from 1870 onwards Victorian acquisitiveness gathered many collections (of which Dutch pictures formed part of a very much larger whole) of very varying quality that ended up in the public domain. This great unevenness of quality has led to the later neglect of such collections.

One of the largest and most interesting was the Bowes Collection, since the 1870s in Barnard Castle, which contained well over a thousand Old Master and 19th-century pictures. Though the Spanish pictures are the best-known part of the collection they are in fact outnumbered by the Dutch. John and Josephine Bowes were apparently unaware of the fact that they possessed a significant group of Dutch 17th-century pictures which included outstanding works by Simon de Vlieger and Adam Willaerts, both very little known at the time. But the number of inferior or damaged works was considerable and this gave the Bowes Collection a bad reputation at the beginning of the 20th century when a critical editorial in the *Burlington Magazine* commented that it was indeed fortunate that the Bowes pictures were not in a centre of large population such as Manchester! The catholicity of the Bowes' taste and their faith in their own judgement is now respected.

Another lesser example is that of the T W Holburne of Menstrie Collection established in Bath in 1872. Again modern research has improved the status of a significant group of pictures proving that Holburne was not without taste – as shown by the number of Holburne paintings included here by Jacob Backer, Nicolaes Berchem, Benjamin Gerritsz. Cuyp, Nicolaes Maes, Cornelis van Poelenburgh and Ary de Vois (see pp.49, 69, 121, 124, 130). The merit of half this collection has been obscured by the rest, many of which remain unidentifiable and are of demonstrably low quality. The Brenchley and Bentlif Collections at Maidstone are similarly mixed.

Far more significant was the Shipley Bequest to Gateshead in 1909. After a massive sale of some two thousand pictures in Newcastle upon Tyne, six hundred works remained to form the permanent collection. The uneven quality of these pictures does not prevent Shipley from emerging as one of the most noteworthy late-Victorian bourgeois whose collection is still partly intact. A painting by Joachim Wttewael (p.43) is that painter's most significant work in the country and several other artists from Shipley's collection are hardly represented in other British collections.

This type of Victorian acquisitiveness had an effect on the collections of the Victoria and Albert Museum which, although never specifically interested in building up a picture collection, had received groups of Dutch pictures via several bequests and among them works of dubious quality.

None of the major municipal collections had set out by 1900 to purchase Dutch pictures on any scale, attention being concentrated on the purchase of contemporary art. Manchester, Leeds, Birmingham, Leicester and Liverpool all opened new picture galleries in the last quarter of the 19th century which were immediately filled with up-to-date pictures. Little interest was shown in the Old Masters and in most cases it was only after 1945 that this emphasis changed. Between the turn of the century and 1945 the growing representation of Dutch paintings in public collections continued to be through the gift of private collections. In 1899 Cheltenham received from the Baron de Ferrieres a collection put together in Belgium some fifty years earlier and, therefore, reflecting mid-19th-century continental taste which had an emphasis on small-scale genre works. Two much grander collections of this type, both put together by members of the Rothschild family, are preserved at Waddesdon Manor and Ascott, both National Trust. In 1904 Nottingham received the Richard Godson Millns Bequest of minor Dutch pictures, mostly of decent quality, whose attributions have not required much revision. The Caird, Ingram and Palmer Collections acquired by the National Maritime Museum, Greenwich, have created there the largest collection of Dutch 17th-century marine paintings in existence both qualitatively and quantitatively. The Broughton Bequest of flower paintings to the Fitzwilliam Museum, Cambridge, made that the largest collection of such works (see pp.68, 111, 148, 149, 153). The Ward Bequest to the Ashmolean Museum, Oxford, in 1940 made that the prime collection of still-life pictures. All these specialist collections of still-life, flower painting and seascapes concentrate on one theme and try to be as comprehensive as possible within that theme. The result can be monotonous and it is worth noting in this context that such a specialist idea did not occur to Dutch collectors in the 17th century.

There have been some major collection bequests since the Second World War. The City Art Gallery, York, received the Lycett Green Gift in 1955. This gift has been consistently underestimated since it contains, among other Dutch pictures, the only work by Dirck van Baburen in the country which is a major example of a Dutch Caravaggesque work. Two further private collections have been given to the public in recent years; the Assheton Bennett Collection to Manchester City Art Gallery (1979) and the Samuel Collection to the Mansion House, City of London (1988). Both were largely formed on the advice of one enlightened dealer, Edward Speelman, and reflect a curiously 19th-century taste in Dutch pictures. In both collections the pictures were chosen for charm of subject, delicacy of lighting, care of brushwork and so on, all aesthetic criteria more typical of the 19th century than of the 20th. Neither collection contains a single major history or religious picture, nor any Mannerist or Caravaggesque works. These two collections therefore reflect the survival of the aesthetic of one age into another just as in the 19th century the Dulwich Collection reflected the tastes of the 18th.

When we turn to collecting by purchase or individual gift, there are some surprises which are likely to reflect the interests of individual curators rather than a general trend. One of the most interesting cities from this point of view is Birmingham, because almost all the Dutch pictures in the two collections (Barber Institute and City Museum and Art Gallery) have been acquired by purchase. No precise taste is detectable and the two institutions have worked independently to build up a group which together still numbers less than forty works. The same is true of Liverpool whose Walker Art Gallery received its most significant Dutch picture, the Rembrandt *Self-Portrait*, as a gift from a local firm. The most notable collection building in this field outside the national collections has been undertaken by the Ferens Museum and Art Gallery, Hull, which has managed by judicious purchase over a period of nearly forty years to build up a good collection of more than average interest (see p.85 for the masterpiece by Frans Hals).

The National Trust has been fortunate to receive four important collections of Dutch pictures, Petworth, Waddesdon Manor and Ascott already mentioned, and Polesden Lacey, an excellent example of Edwardian taste in Dutch pictures.

Today Dutch 17th-century pictures form a significant proportion of the Old Masters held in public hands in the country and given other priorities there can hardly be a case for the wholesale acquisition of many more. Yet British collections remain significantly unbalanced because they continue to depend on 18th- and 19th-century tastes and attitudes. The Dutch in the same period were busy *selling* the pictures which were then held in such high esteem. Hence the survival of such a large number of portraits in Dutch collections, precisely because they were not seen to be valuable enough to sell. Thus only one Dutch group portrait of significance is in a British public collection (p.138). British collectors have usually favoured landscape and due to a change of emphasis by the mid-19th century away from the Italianates towards the naturalist schools both are unusually well-represented in this country. Apart from the specific exceptions of Oxford and Cambridge, still-life and flower paintings are particularly badly represented although such pictures have always had considerable popular appeal. A surprisingly large number of Dutch painters are entirely unrepresented in British public collections, but a high proportion of these are of only local significance and are represented in their town of origin by one or two works only. This is not because some disaster has overtaken pictures by minor and largely imitative artists but because three centuries of constant trading in pictures has led to confused or 'optimistic' attributions. In one celebrated case there has been a dramatic unmasking; Rembrandt's *Landscape with an Obelisk* in the Gardner Museum, Boston, Massachusetts, has been found to have the authentic signature of his pupil Flinck underneath the false 'Rembrandt'. The Royal Collection Vermeer, *Music Lesson*, had a false signature of Pieter de Hooch added in the 18th century although in this instance the optimist did not trouble to remove Vermeer's authentic signature.

The number of Dutch 17th-century pictures which remain in private collections and on the art market is considerable, but few of them could be considered as suitable candidates for a public collection because they are usually slightly inferior examples to what is already there. Seen as a whole, the national priority should be to search for less well-represented artists even though this tends to cut across the needs of an individual collection. Hull has been able to fulfil both criteria adding pictures by Daniel de Blieck and Pieter Janssens Elinga (pp.54, 140) in recent years.

The National Collections have, as might be expected, continued to acquire acknowledged masterpieces such as Edinburgh's Pieter Jansz. Saenredam *Interior of St Bavo, Haarlem* and the National Gallery has acquired in recent years works by Rembrandt, Jan Steen, and Willem Kalf. This has been in tandem with a policy of acquisition of little-known and rare masters such as Pynas, Uyttenbroeck and Cornelis van Haarlem. This has broadened the National Collection significantly. In the present climate only the National Collections have the funds to make expensive purchases and all the less well-endowed institutions will have to continue to acquire on an ad hoc basis.

Seen in a wider context, many aspects of British public collections are the envy of other countries. French public collections have almost no seascapes although they are significantly rich in history paintings. Dutch collections are notoriously weak in such British favourites as Aelbert Cuyp and Meindert Hobbema even though these gaps have been partly remedied in recent years. American public collections, so significant in the work of the great masters, especially Rembrandt, Hals and Vermeer of Delft, have shown little interest in other areas and the whole Dutch holdings hardly measure up to the Old Masters of other schools. Indeed, American museums have been disposing of pictures by minor Dutch masters rather than acquiring them. Both numerically and qualitatively such collections as Cambridge and Glasgow are hardly rivalled in America for their holdings of all but the great masters.